Nuclear Proliferation: Prospects for Control

v

© 1970 by the Dunellen Publishing Company, Inc.
145 East 52nd Street
New York, New York, 10022

International Standard Book Number 0-8424-0011-7

Library of Congress Catalogue Card Number 79-129079

Printed in the United States of America.

Bernhard G. Bechhoefer
David B. Brooks
George Bunn
Joseph I. Coffey
Richard A. Falk
Adrian S. Fisher
Victor Gilinsky
Henry R. Myers
John Gorham Palfrey
George W. Rathjens, Jr.
Lawrence Scheinman
Herbert Scoville, Jr.

Edited by
Bennett Boskey
Mason Willrich

Published for the
American Society
of International
Law

Nuclear Prolifereration: Prospects for Control

UNIVERSITY PRESS OF CAMBRIDGE, MASS. 1639

The Dunellen Company, Inc., New York

Preface

The problems of arms control have continually acquired new dimensions since the dawn of the nuclear age in 1945. A remote doomsday has been replaced by an imminent threat of nuclear annihilation. The urgency of finding practical solutions is now well understood. The idea that partial solutions can be valuable even though they fall far short of perfection has become widely recognized.

The Treaty on the Non-Proliferation of Nuclear Weapons went into force in March, 1970. Treaty negotiations spanned the administrations of Presidents Kennedy, Johnson, and Nixon. Like the Limited Nuclear Test Ban Treaty, it is a significant step toward an accommodation among the nations of the world on nuclear issues—an accommodation that is essential for the survival of mankind. President Nixon has expressed the hope that the Non-Proliferation Treaty will prove to be "one of the first and major steps in that process in which the nations of the world moved from a period of confrontation to a period of negotiation and a period of lasting peace." Premier Kosygin of the Soviet Union and many other world leaders have made similar declarations.

Plainly, some basic changes in the international environment are required if the Non-Proliferation Treaty is to work. The problems that the treaty raises—political, military, technical, and administrative—must be widely understood if they are to be dealt with successfully.

This volume is intended to provide general readers with an appreciation of the Non-Proliferation Treaty's possibilities and problems, as foreseen by a diverse group of highly qualified experts. In 1967 the American Society of

International Law established a Panel on Nuclear Energy and World Order. The members of the panel represent different disciplines—law, the natural sciences, the social sciences—and have had a variety of experience in government, the academic community, research organizations, and private industry. (The present membership is set forth in Appendix E.) It was expected that, by a process of informal discussion among the members of the panel, there would occur a fruitful exchange of viewpoints, bringing new insights to the work of each of the members. It was also hoped that there might be opportunities for encouraging original scholarship and commentary bearing on important public issues.

As it became clear that the Non-Proliferation Treaty was likely to go into effect in the near future, the panel felt that it might be able to foster public understanding of the problem of nuclear proliferation, the scope of the treaty, the possible lines of solutions for the basic issues involved, and the longer-term prospects for the treaty's success or failure. The papers in this volume by various members of the panel were accordingly commissioned after extensive consideration of the areas it would be most useful and important to explore.

The volume is not a committee report in which ideas have been consistently softened to meet a standard of the least common denominator. Rather, it is a collection of essays that have taken into account suggestions by panel members. No effort has been made to have the papers conform to any single mold. They represent a variety of points of view and reflect the diverse experience and knowledge of their authors.

No paper in the volume necessarily represents the views either of the American Society of International Law or of the members of the panel other than the author. At the same time, the panel as a whole does believe that each paper included presents important issues of general interest in a manner that will contribute to better public knowledge and understanding of this complex subject.

On behalf of the panel, we wish to express our appreciation to the American Society of International Law for providing us with this opportunity to serve the public interest. As editors, we also wish to express our particular gratitude to the contributors who gave unstintingly of their time and creative effort in order to bring this volume into existence.

Bennett Boskey,
Chairman of the Panel

Mason Willrich,
Rapporteur of the Panel

Contents

Appendixes

List of Tables and Figures

Part 1 Nuclear Weapons Proliferation

1 Global Dimensions

Adrian S. Fisher

In considering the type of world we are trying to preserve through the Non-Proliferation Treaty, it is well to bear in mind the observation made by the late John F. Kennedy as long ago as July 26, 1963, when he announced that agreement had been reached on a test ban treaty. He said:

> I ask you to stop and think for a moment what it would mean to have nuclear weapons in so many hands, in the hands of countries large and small, stable and unstable, responsible and irresponsible, scattered throughout the world. There would be no rest for anyone then, no stability, no real security and no chance of effective disarmament. There would only be the increased chance of accidental war and an increased necessity for the great powers to involve themselves in what would otherwise be local conflicts.

To avoid such a nightmare world is indeed a desirable objective and, at the present time, the Non-Proliferation Treaty seems a likely instrument to be used in this cause.

In considering the wisdom of our attempts to do so, however, we are often met with the following questions: "How can we expect a nation to sign an agreement to give up the development of a weapons system, such as a nuclear weapons system, which it believes to be essential to its national security? How can we expect a country to live up to such an agreement, even if it signs it, if the development of nuclear weapons should become important to its national security?" Sometimes, if the questioner is of a more moralistic bent, the question is put in the following terms: "What right does the United

States, which is producing nuclear weapons at a rapid rate, have to ask other nations to forgo the very thing that it is doing itself?"

Considering the last of these questions first, the moral right of the United States to urge general accession to the Non-Proliferation Treaty seems established by the fact that when there was only one nuclear weapon state, the United States, we felt that even one was one too many. We made a real effort to insure the complete elimination of nuclear energy from the military field, under effective international control, along the lines of the Acheson-Lilienthal report. We did not do this for altruistic reasons. We did it because we thought it in the best interest of our own security to do so. Had our proposal been accepted in 1946, there would not be five nuclear weapon states today—there would not even be one.

It is fruitless now to cry over spilt milk and go in detail into the reasons for the failure of this effort, as it was developed in the Baruch plan and presented to the United Nations. It is a matter of melancholy history that this proposal did fail. The United States continued to produce increasing numbers of nuclear weapons, the Soviet Union developed and produced its own nuclear weapons, and both of us were doomed to live, for the foreseeable future, in the precarious situation created by the balance of terror. But our efforts to implement the principles of the Acheson-Lilienthal report do give us the moral right to urge signature of a non-proliferation treaty as a means of preventing the situation—which has become increasingly dangerous because there are now five nuclear weapon states—from becoming intolerable by the development of ten or fifteen.

The Non-Proliferation Treaty gives the potential nuclear powers the same opportunity that the United States and the Soviet Union had, and failed to capitalize on, when they failed in the discussions following the presentation of the Baruch plan. There are two facts that support this statement.

The first is that the development of relatively small stockpiles of nuclear weapons by the potential nuclear powers would not be a direct threat to either the United States or the Soviet Union. There is, of course, always the frightening possibility that the United States and the Soviet Union might be dragged into a nuclear conflict growing from nuclear developments somewhere else in the world—say the Middle East or the Indian peninsula. But in an immediate sense, the development of nuclear weapons by a potential nuclear weapon state represents a threat to its neighbors—in many cases also potential nuclear weapon states. And this can be a real threat to peace because the mere possession of nuclear weapons by one nation will tend to create tension, mutual fear, and uncertainty among its neighbors.

There is good reason to believe, from what we have already observed in the Middle East and Southeast Asia, that a non-proliferation treaty will promote rather than diminish the security of the countries in those areas. President Nasser has threatened a preventive war against Israel should it make the decision to acquire nuclear weapons; the Pakistani, fresh from their bitter military encounter with the Indians, have accused them in the United Nations of secretly planning to manufacture nuclear weapons.

Thus no non-nuclear weapon state should feel that it is being asked to sign a non-proliferation treaty as a favor to the nuclear weapon powers. The non-nuclear weapon states might be better advised to feel that the Non-Proliferation Treaty offers them an opportunity to prevent the possibility of their becoming a threat to each other.

Secondly, potential nuclear weapon states should recognize that to the extent any of them feels threatened by the stockpiles of either of the two superpowers, such a threat could be overwhelming. Their own development of nuclear weapons is not apt to provide them with an adequate deterrence against such a threat.

In considering how these states should look to their own security, one must, of course, distinguish between those states which are members of defense alliances and those which are non-aligned. Members of defense alliances will have to look for their protection against nuclear threats to the deterrent effect of their partner in such an alliance and, hopefully, to an increasing accommodation between the two major nuclear powers. It is not clear that the development of an independent nuclear weapons capability would enhance the security of such a state. Indeed, the opposite appears more likely to be the case.

In the case of the Federal Republic of Germany, for example, a decision to develop its own nuclear weapons, with the anticipated Soviet reaction, would not enhance West German security against the threat it may see in the nuclear arsenals and conventional weapons of the Soviet Union—for one reason: it would not be possible, in the foreseeable future, for the West Germans to develop a stockpile of their own that would provide a deterrent against the Soviet threat. Their security is better protected if they look to the stockpile of the United States, together with the strength of the bonds of NATO. That West Germany has signed the treaty and has declared it will ratify, after working out a satisfactory agreement on safeguards, indicates that the preceding argument may now be finding a receptive ear in the Federal Republic of Germany. A similar conclusion may be drawn from the Japanese signature and willingness to ratify.

Countries that are not now members of alliance systems will have to look to the United Nations Security Council Resolution adopted on June 19, 1968, and the statements of intent made by the United States and the Soviet Union at that time. (For further discussion, see Joseph I. Coffey, "Threat,

Reassurance, and Nuclear Proliferation," in this volume.) The full significance of these documents will not be observed by concentration on their *legal* effects but on their *political* effects. This is not a case in which the United States or the Soviet Union has given an indication of its point of view—the action it intends to take under certain conditions—irrespective of the action taken by the other. The important element is that in these limited security assurances the United States and the Soviet Union are taking steps together. This is a political fact with significance that it is hard to overstate. Here we have, in effect, the Soviet Union and the United States together giving an indication that they will react together if India, having signed the Non-Proliferation Treaty, is threatened with nuclear aggression by Communist China. No analysis of the legal effects of the security assurances should be permitted to overshadow this political decision of major proportions.

Many of the potential nuclear powers in considering whether they will become or remain a party to the Non-Proliferation Treaty will of course wish to see how the other parties to the treaty, particularly the United States and the Soviet Union are living up to the obligations of Article VI, which commits all parties to pursue in good faith negotiations relating to a cessation of the arms race and to nuclear disarmament. As a matter of pure military analysis, it might be asked why countries that look to the United States or the Soviet Union (or perhaps both in the case of non-aligned countries concerned about Red China) for their protection against nuclear aggression would be interested in seeing the stockpiles of the superpowers reduced through nuclear disarmament. There are two answers to this question.

The first is a political one. As a practical matter, it is very hard for the political leaders of a country that is capable of developing nuclear weapons, particularly a non-aligned country, to tell its own citizens that it will forswear those weapons through a treaty commitment, while its citizens are aware that the United States and the Soviet Union are producing further nuclear weapons as fast as possible.

This political reason is closely related to the second answer to the military issue that I have raised. While the non-aligned look to the United States and the Soviet Union to protect them against the Chinese, the credibility of any such indication of intent to afford such protection is directly related to the nature of relations between the United States and the Soviet Union. If relations between the two are exacerbated by a continuing nuclear arms race, no non-aligned country could expect either superpower to come to its assistance in the event of a threat from Communist China, because each would be concerned about what the other's reaction might be. On the other hand, if talks on nuclear disarmament, such as the Strategic Arms Limitation Talks, have resulted in a decrease in tensions between the United States and the Soviet Union and an increase in their cooperation with respect to world affairs, the credibility of the security assurances such as those contained in the Security Council Resolution and the accompanying statements is greatly enhanced. This is particularly the case when it is borne in mind that under any disarmament agreement apt to be negotiated in the foreseeable future, the stockpiles of the United States and the Soviet Union will be substantially in excess of that of Communist China.

Our most hopeful hypothesis is that the Non-Proliferation Treaty will obtain global, but not universal dimensions. Communist China is adamantly opposed to the treaty, France has indicated she will not sign (although she will take no action prohibited by the treaty), and one or more potential nuclear weapon states have indicated an unwillingness or reluctance to sign. Does this situation make the treaty a dead letter?

The test of whether the treaty has performed its functions is not limited to whether all potential nuclear weapon states become parties. To the extent that the treaty creates a climate in which a state does not sign for one of a number of reasons but, nevertheless, decides not to develop nuclear weapons, the treaty has fulfilled most of its functions.

In some cases the decision not to acquire nuclear weapons, while refraining from joining the Non-Proliferation Treaty, might be because the country does not wish to change the general climate; this might be the situation in the case of India. In other cases the concern may be over certain specific reactions of others if it should develop nuclear weapons. In the case of Israel, for example, there is probably not too great concern over the Arab threat to wage a preventive war if the Israelis should develop nuclear weapons. But the fact that the Soviet Union might react by making nuclear weapons available to the Arabs—even though the Soviets would doubtless keep custody and control over the weapons—would certainly be a strong deterrent to an Israeli decision to go nuclear.

Finally, there remains the impact of the treaty in leading to the creation of a worldwide—or nearly worldwide—system of controls over the material used in making nuclear weapons. Article III of the treaty provides for the establishment of international safeguards to see that material supplied by parties to any non-nuclear weapon state—including non-parties—is not diverted to make a bomb or other explosive device. This means that non-parties to the treaty will have to look solely to their own indigenous material—or material obtained from other non-parties—if they intend to develop nuclear weapons. It will be complicated even if such material is available because, if they retain relations with the major suppliers who are parties to the treaty, the safeguards required by the treaty on the nuclear fuel cycle will probably give some indication that indigenous materials (or materials obtained from non-parties) are being channeled into weapons.

Therefore, it seems possible that a non-proliferation treaty of global—but not necessarily universal—dimensions can be a truly meaningful document. Under it the questions asked at the beginning of this article might be rephrased as follows: "In view of the regime established by the widespread acceptance of the Non-Proliferation Treaty, doesn't it enhance a nation's long-range security interests to sign such an agreement? Wouldn't it be in its security interests to live up to such an agreement?"

It is submitted that—on balance—the answer to these two questions is in the affirmative.

2 Constraints on the Nuclear Arms Race

George W. Rathjens, Jr.

Technological Developments

In considering the problems of vertical nuclear proliferation—that is, the enhancement of nuclear capabilities of those nations already possessing nuclear weapons—it is appropriate first to discuss the technological options in the field of strategic weapons that are of concern in the 1970's. In so doing, one may concentrate largely on the trends that seem likely in the Soviet Union and the United States. After all, with some exceptions, the possibility is remote that the other three nuclear powers—or others that might emerge—will develop and deploy systems or use technologies different from those of the superpowers. Rather, the technology and the systems on which the lesser powers will focus their attention will, to the extent they are sophisticated, emulate those of the United States and the Soviet Union.

The early 1970's will clearly be a period of considerable change in Soviet and American strategic force postures unless the Strategic Arms Limitation Talks (SALT) produce early and comprehensive agreement. Two developments are of particular concern: antiballistic missile (ABM) defenses and multiple independently targetable re-entry vehicles (MIRV's).

ABM's

ABM defense of sorts was a technological possibility throughout the 1960's, and the United States spent many hundreds of millions of dollars attempting to develop an effective system. The Soviet Union went further. After early

abortive attempts, a very limited ABM system was deployed around Moscow.
Several considerations make the prospects for ABM defense greater and more
troublesome during the 1970's.

First, there are technological developments. Phased array radars, which
involve steering the radar beam electronically, make it possible now for a
single radar, in conjunction with sophisticated computers, to track and make
measurements on many objects arriving nearly simultaneously. This was not
possible with the older radars, which required the mechancial slewing of large
antennas. Moreover, development of interceptor missiles, capable of very high
accelerations, now makes it possible to defer the decision to launch interceptors until adversary warheads have penetrated the upper layers of the
atmosphere. Such delay permits the defense to capitalize on the fact that
many penetration aids, which would otherwise be confused with actual
warheads, will interact differently with the atmosphere than warheads. This
makes it possible for the defense to concentrate its destructive efforts against
the actual warhead re-entry vehicles. Finally, the development of high yield
defensive warheads that produce very high fluxes of X-rays requires that
offensive warheads be separated by rather large distances prior to re-entry
into the atmosphere in order to prevent the possibility of the destruction of
several by a single defensive burst.

Second, the prospective growth of nuclear capabilities by other powers,
particularly China, provides an impetus for Soviet and American ABM deployment that was not relevant during the 1960's. The prevailing view in the
United States throughout that period was that an attempt to defend American population and industrial capacity against a determined Soviet missile
attack would be essentially hopeless. Any defense would be offset by a
compensating, or possibly even more-than-compensating, improvement in
Soviet offensive capabilities. This view still prevails, which explains the
rejection of proposals for the deployment of a large-scale American ABM
defense system. Although one cannot be certain, the Soviet failure to complete the defenses around Moscow and extend them may be due to a belated
acceptance of a similar view about the futility of defense against American
capabilities. The problems of defense against a lesser nuclear power are less
difficult, however, and it is likely that both the United States and the Soviet
Union could build an ABM defense that would be effective for some years in
reducing the damage that might be inflicted by a smaller nuclear power.

Third, the development of MIRV's and improvements in missile accuracy
make it likely that fixed facilities, and in particular hardened ICBM sites, can
be destroyed by a pre-emptive missile attack even if there are fewer attacking
missiles than targets. With this development, specialized ABM defenses have
been proposed for still another role: the defense of missile sites to reduce the

effectiveness of such a pre-emptive attack, or to make it at least a much less predictable operation.

Actually, for several reasons such a defense presents far fewer technical problems than defending industry and population. First, in the case of missile sites, nearby nuclear bursts that would destroy a city can be tolerated. Thus the defense can defer a decision to intercept an object until it is fairly near the target and need not intercept at all those objects that can be expected to miss the target by about a mile. Second, a pre-emptive attack against an adversary's ICBM force would probably be rejected as too dangerous unless the offense had assurance that it would destroy nearly all of the missiles it was attacking. This means that the defenses need not necessarily be highly effective to serve as a deterrent. They serve a useful purpose simply by introducing uncertainty about the outcome of the attack. Third, the defense can tolerate the loss of many of its ICBM's and can therefore decide to concentrate its efforts on the defense of a few, while the offense must attack them all.

In defending cities against a missile attack, the situation would generally be the reverse. The defense would want high confidence in its effectiveness and want to defend all major cities. The offense, on the other hand, might feel it needs to destroy only a limited number of cities to deliver an effective retaliatory strike or to have the kind of effective deterrent that such a retaliatory capability would imply.

MIRV's

The United States is now engaged in programs to equip both its land- and sea-based missiles with MIRV's designed primarily to facilitate penetration of any possible Soviet ABM system. This concept involves the delivery by a single rocket of several warheads each of which can be directed to a separate target. By greatly multiplying the number of warheads against which the defense will have to commit interceptors, the offense can have higher confidence in being able to penetrate defenses than if each missile carries only a single warhead and decoys designed to simulate warheads.

Simple multiple warheads—those that cannot be individually directed to separate targets—are much less effective than MIRV's, for if the spacing between simple multiple warheads is so small that they will strike in the same general target area, e.g., a large city, it may be possible, for the reasons discussed earlier, to destroy them all with a single high yield, high altitude interceptor. With MIRV's, however, the defense can be denied that possibility since several warheads carried by a single rocket can begin to separate early in the missile trajectory to go to different targets. By the time they might possibly be intercepted, they will be widely separated in space.

The United States has been testing MIRV's for some time and has begun the conversion of some Polaris submarines so that they can accommodate the larger Poseidon missile that will carry MIRV's. The first generation of United States MIRV's will have yields in the range of tens of kilotons and accuracy measured within a fraction of a mile. They will be highly effective for penetrating possible Soviet defenses, but the yield-accuracy combination is not expected to be good enough to make them very useful for destroying Soviet hardened ICBM's. However, improving the accuracy by a factor of two, which could probably be achieved in a few years, would reduce the number of missiles required for attacking hardened targets by a factor of four. United States MIRV's would then provide a "hard-target" kill capability.

The Soviet multiple warhead program is probably less advanced technically than that of the United States and may not even involve independently targetable re-entry vehicles. In fact, present evidence suggests that the Soviet multiple warhead system now being tested may not be able to achieve large separation distances between warheads carried by the same rocket. Thus the system may be similar to the presently operational United States Polaris A-3 missile, which can deliver several warheads that are not independently targetable. The Soviet multiple warhead, however, could carry yields as much as 50 or 100 times as great as those that will be carried by the first generation of United States MIRV's. Thus a hard-target kill capability may be achievable with relatively poor accuracy.

Unfortunately, MIRV's and improvements in their guidance will raise the specter of either side's being able to destroy virtually all of the adversary's missile sites as well as other fixed installations in a surprise attack. Yet a few ICBM's might survive such an attack. In addition, other components of the retaliatory force, in particular submarine-launched missiles, would also survive. Since a devastating retaliatory blow would still, therefore, be possible, the author would not be greatly concerned about the prospect of a surprise attack delivered by a MIRV missile force. Many others, however, are very perturbed about such a possibility—so much so that it seems likely undefended ICBM sites will be considered obsolete by the end of the 1970's, assuming MIRV technology is developed and missile accuracies continue to improve as they have in the past.

So far, no promising method of extending the life of fixed ICBM's in a MIRV era is in sight. Superhardening of missile sites would be no more than a palliative since increasing the blast resistance of a hardened site by a factor of five could be offset by an improvement in MIRV accuracy by a factor of two. An ABM defense may not be very useful either. If MIRV accuracy is improved by a factor of two, the warhead size required to destroy a given facility will drop considerably. This will make it possible for a rocket of a given size to carry about three times as many effective warheads, thus greatly complicating the defense problem.

The MIRV-ABM Interaction

MIRV's and ABM's can each serve two very different purposes; this results in their having a particularly pernicious effect on the Soviet-American strategic arms race and on efforts to control it. MIRV's may be used to facilitate penetration of ABM defenses, thereby enhancing retaliatory or deterrent capability, or they may be used in a so-called first strike to weaken the adversary's ability to retaliate. Although the technical requirements, especially regarding accuracy, will differ somewhat in the two cases, a particular MIRV system may be useful, or at least appear to be, for either purpose. And, of course, in its reaction to the development of weapons capabilities by its adversary, each side will place the most pessimistic construction possible on any ambiguity about its adversary's capabilities or intentions.

ABM defenses as well may give rise to ambiguity. It is technically possible to develop and deploy a missile site defense that would be useless for population defense. However, only recently have such specialized defenses commanded much attention. Accordingly, missile site defenses are quite likely to have some capability for population defense and also provide the starting point for construction of an extensive population defense within a shorter period of time than if population defenses had to be developed without this foundation.

The American Safeguard ABM system clearly has these qualities. It may be construed as an attempt to limit the Soviet Union's retaliatory capability against American population or at least to foreshadow the building of a defense for that purpose. Safeguard may thus be interpreted as an attempt to make more feasible a United States first strike, for with an ABM defense of population there would be some hope of coping with most of those adversary missiles not destroyed by pre-emptive attack.

One is thus confronted with the following possibilities:

1. If one side deploys a defense of population, or is thought to be about to do so because of its research and development program or public announcements or because it is deploying a defense of missile sites that is subject to ambiguous interpretation, the other will feel compelled to develop and deploy MIRV's to facilitate penetration of the defense.

2. If one side deploys MIRV's, no matter what their actual purpose, the other side will view them as a possible threat to the retaliatory capability of its fixed ICBM's. It will feel compelled either to defend its ICBM's or to procure other capabilities that will not be similarly vulnerable These might

include, among others, increased numbers of missile launching submarines, land mobile ICBM's, and advanced aircraft with associated air-to-surface missiles.

Controlling ABM's and MIRV's

The immediate goal in limiting the Soviet-American strategic arms race is to break the action-reaction chain. If ABM's of all kinds could be prevented, there would be no need to acquire MIRV's to penetrate defenses. If development and deployment of highly accurate MIRV's could be prevented, there would be little need to build defenses for ICBM's, assuming comparable force levels on the two sides. Because offensive missiles are neither perfectly reliable nor accurate, one could always be sure that a significant number would survive an attack by a force of comparable size.

The problem may be made vastly more complex if either superpower decides it must build defenses to limit the damage it might suffer at the hands of one of the smaller nuclear powers. An ABM system deployed by one side to cope with a possible Chinese attack, perhaps not even adequate for that purpose, may be perceived by the other as a possible threat to its retaliatory capabilities or as the basis for a defense that could be. This would very likely be the case in the event of an anti-Chinese defense deployed by the United States, since the required radars would also be useful for defense against a Soviet attack. A likely result would be a substantial strengthening of Soviet strategic forces that might well include the deployment of MIRV's.

As for an anti-Chinese system deployed by the Soviet Union, the radars required could be unambiguously ineffective against American ICBM's. Even such an ABM deployment, however, might stimulate a further expansion in United States offensive capabilities. Such a United States reaction would be even more likely if the Soviet radars had omnidirectional capabilities.

Very similar arguments would apply to antisubmarine capabilities. They too will be viewed as unpredictable in their effectiveness (although in this case there would be less room for claiming good performance under any circumstances than for ABM or air defenses). Although their capability would range from very poor to ineffective, ASW capabilities considered by one superpower as somewhat useful in coping with an nth country's missile-launching submarine threat would probably cause the other superpower to strengthen its submarine-launched missile and other retaliatory capabilities.

Designs for Curtailing the Soviet-American Strategic Arms Race

Freeze on Offensive and Defensive Capabilities

The foregoing demonstrates that large-scale deployment of ABM defenses will almost certainly lead to the introduction of MIRV's. MIRV's will lead to

ABM defense of missile sites, or substantial changes in the strategic offensive forces with reduced emphasis on fixed ICBM's, or both. Thus the key to freezing the Soviet-American balance at a level comparable to that existing at present will be prevention of both large-scale ABM defense and MIRV deployment. Of these, the latter is most urgent although fundamentally less important.

The urgency derives from the status of present test programs and the problems of verifying compliance with any agreement banning MIRV deployment. Once the test programs have been completed, it is unlikely that the superpowers could reach an agreement permitting each to verify that the other was not deploying MIRV's. The requirements would be too intrusive, probably requiring on-site inspection, at least on a sampling basis, of adversary missile warheads.

On the other hand, unilateral intelligence techniques would probably suffice to ascertain the occurrence of test firing of missiles equipped with MIRV's. Thus, the best hope of preventing MIRV's from becoming part of strategic weapon arsenals lies in preventing the completion of test programs. Confidence that the adversary was not completing a MIRV program could be heightened if an agreement prohibited not only testing of multiple warheads, but also the testing of decoys and other ABM penetration aids designed to be effective far down into the atmosphere. It would also be useful if the number of tests of conventional ICBM's were restricted by agreement to rather low levels, if each test as well as space flight was announced in advance, and if test firings of missiles were conducted only on ranges that were located so that re-entry could be monitored by the adversary. It is the author's opinion that with such provisions each side could have sufficient confidence in its ability to ascertain whether or not its adversary was complying with an agreement not to test MIRV's.

A few months hence, research and development tests, at least on the first generation American MIRV's, may be essentially completed. But even the United States planners will want additional firings to establish the operational parameters of the system—that is, reliability and accuracy—as well as a continuing program of occasional firings in order to maintain confidence in the system. Accordingly, a prohibition on testing some months hence might still induce the United States not to deploy MIRV's, and would certainly be a powerful inhibition on their ever being used for pre-emptive attack, since this requires extraordinarily high confidence. This would be true even if accuracy could be improved with the testing of single re-entry vehicles. However, Soviet confidence that the United States will not deploy an effective counter-force MIRV system would be lower than if test programs were stopped earlier. The reverse is also true. United States confidence that the Soviets will not deploy MIRV's will be higher if testing can be stopped sooner.

The threat of large-scale ABM deployment, for which MIRV's may be judged necessary penetration aids, need not inhibit either side from agreeing to at least a temporary moratorium on MIRV testing. Should evidence develop that either country was beginning a nationwide ABM defense, the other's MIRV program could be reactivated and carried to the point where effective penetration-aid MIRV's would be available well before the completion of the ABM system in question.

The other essential ingredients of any agreement to freeze the Soviet-American strategic balance would be limitations on numbers of strategic offensive missiles or launchers, and possibly of bombers, as well as controls on ABM deployment. Fortunately, the problems of verifying compliance with limitations on numbers of offensive missile launchers and bombers is easier than in the case of MIRV's. Unilateral intelligence techniques should suffice to determine quite precisely the number of ICBM launchers, missile launching submarines, and strategic bombers.

Estimating the capabilities of an ABM system may be more difficult. Indeed, if large-phased array radars were deployed throughout either the Soviet Union or the United States, the problem could, for reasons discussed later, become very difficult. However, if an agreement could be reached prohibiting any ABM deployment or limiting it to approximately the level of the Moscow defenses or Phase I of Safeguard, then one could have high assurance that a nationwide defense could not be deployed without very substantial advance indication.

Asymmetric Limitations

Agreements less constraining than that outlined above are also possible and, at this late date in terms of MIRV testing, perhaps more likely. If MIRV testing and deployment cannot be prevented, agreement would almost necessarily have to permit replacement of fixed ICBM's by mobile systems, either land- or sea-based. Such an agreement would imply continuing large expenditures for some time, and a major restructuring of strategic forces so that each side would rely less on fixed land-based missiles. The problem would be more difficult for the Soviet Union than for the United States because a much larger fraction of its total retaliatory capability is in fixed ICBM's.

This suggests the possibility of an asymmetric agreement, although in its extreme form this is probably of no more than academic interest. If the Soviet Union depended for deterrence primarily on a very large ICBM force and the United States on a small submarine missile force, and assuming no urban ABM on either side, there would seem to be no reason for either to be concerned about a first strike by the other. The Soviet ICBM force would probably have to be permitted to grow as United States MIRV technology improved, or the Soviet missile sites would have to be defended with specialized "hard-point" ABM defenses, or both. Otherwise, the United States submarine missiles, even though smaller in number than the Soviet ICBM force, would eventually be capable of an effective first strike. Because of the relative lack of secrecy in the United States, the Soviet Union could probably always estimate with reasonable precision the counterforce capability of the United States submarine fleet. It could, therefore, increase the number of ICBM's or defend them as required, even denouncing the agreement if need be in order to strengthen its retaliatory capability sufficiently. To persuade the United States to rely for deterrence entirely on a submarine force of rather limited size, it might be necessary for the Soviet Union to agree to greatly curtail or abandon its ASW efforts, which the United States could probably monitor unilaterally with adequate assurance.

The scheme is a bit unrealistic because it would require abandoning certain programs, thus reducing present capabilities substantially. Also one side or the other would probably be unwilling to rely for deterrence on a single system. Furthermore, the United States would very likely find it politically unacceptable to agree to the Soviet Union's having a much larger missile force than it has.

Limitations on Missile Payload

Still another formula for dealing with the MIRV problem has been suggested. This involves setting limits on the total missile payload that can be delivered, leaving it to each side to decide for itself the extent to which MIRV's would be deployed—the more MIRV's per missile, the smaller the yield of each and for that matter the smaller the aggregate yield. Implicit in the proposal is the assumption that each side could determine, by unilateral techniques, whether major configurational changes were being made that would permit a significant increase in payload—probably a reasonable assumption. While the number of MIRV's that could be carried by a given missile may be quite uncertain, the hard-target kill capability of the missile will not change much if the number of MIRV's is somewhat greater or smaller than optimum. Accordingly, if one can estimate with some precision the accuracy, reliability, and payload of the adversary's missiles, it should be possible to place a fairly exact upper limit on their hard-target kill capability. But the "if" that is involved is large indeed. As noted earlier, kill capability is extremely sensitive to accuracy, and it may be very difficult to estimate the latter. In fact, the adversary may not even have a precise idea of his own missile accuracy.

Uncertainty in adversary capabilities, however, is probably not the most serious objection to such a proposal. Rather, the proposal does not touch upon the fundamental problem raised by MIRV's—the possibility that with them it may be possible for a given number of missiles to destroy with high confidence an equal or even larger number of adversary missiles. This possibility will be realized if MIRV technology and accuracy improve. Agreements limiting total payload for each side can at most delay the day. When that day arrives or even before, both sides may well become concerned about the adversary striking first, and will therefore feel impelled to defend their fixed ICBM's or, more likely, to build up their mobile forces.

An agreement to limit payloads, therefore, cannot be expected to prevent the obsolescence of fixed undefended ICBM's nor the major expenditures and the changes in the strategic forces of both sides that will result from that obsolescence. Limitation on total payload may still be a desirable component of an agreement. However, it should be regarded not as a solution to the MIRV problem, but simply as a device for establishing limits on offensive forces and for permitting substitutions of one kind of missile for another.

It has occasionally been suggested that such a formula should be extended to permit each side to include both ABM interceptors and offensive missiles in a single quota on numbers of missiles or on total payload. Yet this suggestion fails to reflect the fact that at present the best hope for controlling ABM systems lies in limiting radars rather than missile deployment. The radars and their associated computers are the largest components in an ABM system and require the longest construction time. Thus one can best ascertain whether nationwide ABM deployment is being undertaken by looking for radar construction.

Indeed, it is quite possible to envisage an ABM system relying primarily or entirely on fairly small mobile interceptors, about the size of Sprints or smaller. In that case it might not be possible to estimate at all accurately the number of interceptors in the system. (The present relaxed view about being able to monitor adversary strategic missile strength is based not on ability to count the missiles themselves, but rather ICBM launchers and missile launching submarines.)

Strategic Force Reductions

Regrettably, the most that can probably be expected of an early Soviet-American arms agreement would be a freeze or a curtailment of growth of strategic forces. But it is not too early to begin to consider reduction as well. There would be problems, although not insurmountable, as to equivalence of Soviet and American missiles and aircraft. Limiting total payload for each side might be one solution.

With a reduction scheme residual forces would be fairly large pending the negotiation of broad agreements that would affect tactical nuclear capabilities of the superpowers and, for that matter, the capabilities of all of the other nuclear powers as well. With modest reductions, verification would not be much more difficult than for a simple freeze.

In order to minimize the first-strike problem it seems clear that any agreement for reduction of strategic force levels should permit, and possibly encourage, preferential reduction of fixed land-based systems and probably of strategic bombers as well.

ABM Constraints

The foregoing discussion of possible agreements to limit the strategic capabilities of the superpowers has been predicated on their seeing no need to deploy defenses to limit possible damage from other nuclear powers. Should they feel such defense is necessary, the prospects for damping down the Soviet-American arms race will be much diminished. The only apparent hope then would be a degree of collaboration between them that seems remote, at least for a few years.

Each could, for example, deploy an ABM system designed to cope with a possible missile attack by lesser powers, but with the number of interceptors being small enough so as to be unambiguously ineffective in thwarting a retaliatory blow by the other superpower. Yet in order to assure confidence in compliance with an agreement permitting such deployment, broad and intrusive inspection arrangements would be essential. Both sides would have to be assured not only that the number of the adversary's interceptor missiles conformed to the agreement, but also that there was no existing capability for further rapid production.

Construction of ABM systems unambiguously incapable of coping with the sophisticated penetration aids and tactics that the superpowers might employ—for example, systems relying exclusively on exoatmospheric interception—would obviously pose the same kinds of problems. Whether the agreed limits were quantitative, qualitative, or both, the situation would be a dynamic one. In the first instance, the number of interceptors would have to be increased continually. In the second, the general performance characteristics of the system would have to be improved in a carefully controlled way—just enough to keep ahead of presumably ever improving and enlarging nth country threats, and yet not so rapidly so as to be effective against the other superpower's retaliatory capability. One could of course envisage far more collaboration involving joint Soviet-American design, construction, and manning of defense systems to cope with possible nth country threats.

What it all comes down to is the probability, at least in the near term, that the United States and the Soviet Union will soon have to choose among the following alternatives: (1) setting aside desires to construct defenses against the Chinese and other emerging powers; (2) accepting inspection or collaboration with respect to their defenses of a kind not acceptable even during World War II; or (3) continuing their arms race with no significant limitations.

The discussion up to this point has been concerned exclusively with the kinds of issues that can be expected to receive consideration in connection with the Strategic Arms Limitation Talks. However, SALT-type agreements may not be the only ones that would affect the growth of the strategic arsenals of the superpowers. Three others merit at least brief comment: a comprehensive nuclear test ban, agreement to cut off or limit the production of fissionable materials for weapons purposes, and the Nuclear Non-Proliferation Treaty.

Comprehensive Nuclear Test Ban

At present, the United States is engaged in a program of nuclear tests directly related to developing warheads for new weapons systems. For example, it is proposed that some very large-yield nuclear tests be conducted at Amchitka in the Aleutian Islands in connection with the development of a warhead for the Spartan ABM missile. The Soviet Union is also presumably carrying out tests related to the development of warheads for new strategic weapons. But the nature of systems designs and the effectiveness of new American and Soviet strategic systems would not likely be much prejudiced by inability to complete such tests. For example, with respect to ABM systems, the uncertainties that could be resolved as a result of nuclear tests, and especially underground nuclear tests, will be dwarfed by those that remain. Moreover, with a prohibition of all further tests, somewhat more conservative weapons designs would in some cases be adopted. The results would be increases in costs or reductions in effectiveness by a few percent. Assuming these judgments to be correct, it would seem unlikely that a comprehensive nuclear test ban treaty could have a seriously inhibiting effect on the Soviet-American strategic arms race. On the other hand, as long as it remains highly likely that new systems will be deployed, there will be pressure from the weapons systems designers to carry out nuclear tests related to the new systems. Thus, the failure to reach an agreement to limit strategic armaments is likely also to make impossible a comprehensive test ban agreement.

Fissionable Material Production Cut-off

A cut-off in fissionable material production for weapons purposes (and possible reductions in nuclear materials devoted to weapons as well) was during the late fifties and early sixties a seriously considered possibility for controlling the Soviet-American arms race. However, such proposals no longer command much attention. By the midsixties it seemed that a cut-off would have little effect. Tactical nuclear weapons, because of their large numbers, required large amounts of fissionable materials. With the growth in nuclear stockpiles there was undoubtedly a several-fold excess over strategic requirements in the case of both the United States and the Soviet Union, especially since interest in tactical weapons has now waned. In addition, verification problems and lack of Soviet interest in fissionable materials limitations made it unlikely that any agreement could be reached.

With the introduction of MIRV's and ABM the situation may be somewhat different in the 1970's. Once the superpowers start down these paths, and particularly if either makes an attempt to deploy an ABM system to defend its population against a massive attack by the other, the requirements for fissionable materials for strategic systems could increase manyfold. Yet, the stockpiles are now so large, including materials presently incorporated in thousands of tactical nuclear weapons, that really major increases in numbers of strategic weapons or drastic agreed reductions in nuclear stockpiles, or both, would be required before fissionable materials limitations would affect strategic programs significantly. That fact, along with continuing problems of verification, suggests that an attempt to constrain the strategic arms race by limiting fissionable materials stockpiles would not likely be fruitful.

Non-Proliferation Treaty Constraints on Superpowers

Article VI of the Non-Proliferation Treaty requires the superpowers "to pursue negotiations in good faith on effective measures relating to cessation of the nuclear arms race at an early date and to nuclear disarmament." Clearly this article was included in an effort to meet the objections of potential nuclear powers that the treaty is discriminating and that it imposes important limitations on the freedom of action of non-nuclear powers but no correspondingly important constraints on the nuclear powers. The existence of this article and the fact that significant progress by the superpowers in reaching agreement to control their strategic armaments might induce an increased number of accessions to the treaty certainly provide some impetus for the United States and the Soviet Union to reach a SALT agreement.

However, in the author's cynical view there is likely, in fact, to be almost no coupling between the problem of controlling nuclear proliferation among the have-nots and controlling the strategic arms growth of the superpowers. The one non-nuclear weapon state about which there has been greatest concern, the Federal Republic of Germany, is in the process of becoming party to the Non-Proliferation Treaty. The positions of most of the others, about whom there continues to be concern, are not likely to be much influenced by Soviet-American progress in SALT. It is true that a superpower agreement might have a slightly salutary effect in inhibiting nuclear proliferation among such states as Japan, India, Pakistan, the United Arab Republic, and Israel. Soviet-American progress on SALT might be seen as suggesting an increased likelihood that the superpowers might act in concert to preserve peace in the Near East or South Asia. But other considerations would be more important—the actions of China in the case of Japan and India, and local tensions and great power support or lack thereof in both the Near East and South Asia.

The probability that the positions of these states with respect to nuclear proliferation will not be greatly influenced by SALT progress must realistically be viewed as reducing to negligible proportions whatever impetus to SALT one might have hoped there would be from the non-proliferation effort—an impetus in any case dwarfed by bilateral Soviet-American considerations and by concerns of each of the superpowers about China.

Influencing the Strategic Programs of the Medium Nuclear Powers

In the longer run it might be hoped that China, France, and Great Britain will be parties to agreements to limit nuclear strength, although certainly in the case of China, and possibly in the case of France, the time may be some years off. In considering how realistic that hope might be, it is important first to examine the motives of these nations for acquiring and maintaining strategic nuclear capabilities. The desire for national prestige, for a greater voice in international diplomacy, for the possibility of using nuclear strength or the threat thereof against other medium and small powers, and for deterring attack by the superpowers are all plausible motivations.

The last consideration has almost certainly been a major one for China. To some degree it has also influenced France, and possibly even Great Britain. Building capabilities adequate for this last purpose may well be a more difficult problem for the medium powers than building those to meet the other objectives. Indeed, it has frequently been argued, by Robert McNamara and McGeorge Bundy among others, that the disparity in industrial capacity and the other elements of strength between the superpowers, on the one hand, and all other nations, on the other, is so great as to make futile any efforts by the latter to acquire nuclear capabilities significant in terms of Soviet or American standards. And other Americans in responsible positions, for instance John Foster, presently Director of Defense Research and Engineering, have argued that it is within the capability of first the Sentinel and now the Safeguard ABM system to *deny* damage to the United States from a Chinese attack. President Nixon himself has stated that an anti-Chinese defense would be "virtually infallible."

It is the author's view that such denigration of nth country nuclear potential is based partly on wishful thinking, partly on an unwarranted underestimation of the damage-inflicting capability of nuclear weapons, and partly on misplaced confidence in the infallibility of technology. The Chinese have already tested nuclear devices with yields of about three megatons, 200 times that of those used on Hiroshima and Nagasaki. This does not mean that such weapons would inflict 200 times the damage that the first United States atomic weapons caused—30 to 40 times the damage might be a better approximation. In any case, the prospect of even one such weapon being delivered against large Soviet or American cities would be a powerful deterrent to any action by the superpowers that could conceivably provoke such a response.

Damage from an nth country attack could probably be greatly reduced either by intercepting the attacking missiles or by forcing the country in question to use precious payload capability for penetration aids. But the fact remains that there would be an urgent requirement for constant upgrading of defenses to cope with nth country threats that would continually increase in size and sophistication. Furthermore, one could never be confident that the defense would be highly effective, let alone infallible. The superpowers may find themselves surprised by the nature of penetration aids being used; an nth country attack may be concentrated against one or two areas, saturating or exhausting the defenses in those particular locations; there is a probability, by no means remote, that the defenses would fail altogether. In short, there is a very good chance that at least some nuclear weapons originating from a small nuclear power could penetrate any Soviet or American defenses.

This would hold true even if the Soviet Union or the United States pre-emptively attacked, for example, the Chinese nuclear delivery system. Such an attack would probably be nearly 100 percent effective in destroying any missiles on the ground, leaving at most a few for an ABM defense to engage. However, neither superpower could ever launch a pre-emptive attack with certainty that Chinese missiles would not be launched before the impact of American or Soviet missiles. Moreover, a pre-emptive Soviet or American attack could well be ineffective if China should emulate the other four nuclear powers and build a submarine-based nuclear force. One may conclude that the medium nuclear powers are capable of a certain amount of deterrence vis-à-vis the United States and the Soviet Union.

When considering the possibility of inducing the lesser powers either to give up their nuclear programs or to modify them significantly, it is apparent that the prospects vary considerably from one power to the other. Soviet construction of a large-scale ABM system might induce the United Kingdom and France to abandon efforts to maintain nuclear forces. Or, the United States might exploit such a Soviet move by offering its allies advice and assistance with respect to penetration aids to compensate for Soviet defenses, demanding in return modifications in British and French nuclear weapons policy. On the other hand, if the United States were to build a large-scale defense for population, the rationale would presumably be a high degree of effectiveness—much higher than now seems attainable. In that case, several U.S. allies, Britain and France included, might well appeal to the United States for assistance in building ABM defenses of their own. The United States would then be in a position to demand renunciation of nuclear offensive capabilities in exchange for such help.

Even assuming neither superpower deploys large-scale ABM defenses, there would still be some mechanisms available for affecting British, and to a lesser degree French, nuclear programs. These would include (1) economic inducements, (2) modifications in their role in alliance policy, (3) possible changes in U.S. deployment of military forces in Europe and U. S. policy with respect to the employment of tactical nuclear weapons, and (4) removal by the Soviet Union of MRBM/IRBM's from western Russia. It is, however, probably unrealistic to expect that the United States and the Soviet Union unilaterally or jointly would adopt policies with respect to these matters that would induce the United Kingdom, let alone France, to give up nuclear weapons aspirations. The advantage to either superpower would not be great enough to justify paying a heavy price for British or French renunciation.

Both superpowers would obviously pay a much higher price in the case of China. Yet at this point there is probably nothing that could prevent the Chinese from continuing their development of nuclear delivery capabilities (with the possible exception of a nuclear attack against them). This is not to say that the Chinese nuclear program cannot be influenced by Soviet-American actions. Development of ABM defenses by the superpowers would probably result in an acceleration of the Chinese program. Moves in the direction of Soviet-American rapprochement might have similar effects.

Conclusion

To conclude, it seems that it is still possible for the United States and the Soviet Union to freeze their strategic forces at present levels. Neither would risk much by doing so and both would benefit greatly.

The problem of preventing MIRV development is rapidly becoming more difficult, and unless testing and deployment are stopped very soon, the problem will probably be insurmountable. In that case it may still be possible to limit Soviet and American strategic forces, but large expenditures and quite different force structures would become necessary as the obsolescence of fixed land-based missiles became recognized.

Whether or not MIRV testing and deployment is stopped, any superpower agreement would necessarily have to prevent the growth of large-scale ABM defenses of population. Unless the superpowers are able to cooperate to a degree not now foreseeable, it will probably be impossible to maintain limitations on their strategic offensive systems if either or both deploy defenses designed to cope with a nuclear attack by one of the other present nuclear powers. Since such defenses are likely to be ineffective anyway, at least in the sense of permitting the superpowers greater freedom of action in dealing with the other nuclear powers, they would lose little by forswearing them.

The possibility that superpower pressure could be effective in inducing China to forgo the acquisition of a strategic nuclear force seems remote. Chinese accession during the next few years to any agreement that would constrain its growth as a nuclear power seems equally unlikely. The French and British nuclear programs are likely to be more susceptible to limitations by agreement or as a result of pressure from the superpowers. But in these cases superpower pressure is not likely to be very strong simply because there is not great concern.

A Postscript on the Tactical Nuclear Problem

The foregoing has focused almost entirely on strategic nuclear capabilities. However, the problem of tactical and dual-purpose nuclear systems merits at least brief comment.

Some of the dual-purpose delivery systems of the United States and the Soviet Union could be used not only for tactical purposes, but also to deliver nuclear weapons in a strategic role against population, industry, and strategic weapons installations. This is true of the carrier task forces of the United States and some of the tactical aircraft deployed in Europe, which could deliver "tactical" nuclear weapons against the Soviet Union, and Soviet medium-range bombers, which could be used against the United States. Furthermore, the IRBM's, MRBM's, and many of the shorter range bombers of the Soviet Union could be used in a strategic role against the Western European and Asian allies of the United States.

If these delivery systems had a significant counterforce capability against the pure strategic forces of either side, they would clearly loom large in any consideration of strategic arms limitations. Fortunately, they do not because of limited range or relatively long flight times.

Tactical nuclear capabilities would also be important in the context of arms agreements involving drastic reductions in strategic weapons. But the present overkill capability of pure strategic systems is so large that the reductions would have to be drastic indeed before the dual-purpose and intermediate-range systems would have to be included in any agreement. Even reductions as high as 90 percent in pure strategic capabilities would leave each superpower with the capacity to devastate the other totally. For these reasons, the problems of limiting the Soviet-American strategic arms race and tactical nuclear capabilities can hopefully be treated as separable.

Nevertheless, the existence, present deployment, and possible further spread of tactical nuclear capabilities are all troublesome and important concerns for those interested in nuclear proliferation and arms controls. The role that tactical nuclear weapons may play in world affairs is ill-defined and contentious. They may, of course, be used tactically against a non-nuclear power by either the United States or the Soviet Union. However, with each passing year of non-use that seems increasingly unlikely.

Perhaps the major role tactical nuclear weapons play is simply to help bridge the firepower gap between conventional combat and intercontinental strategic nuclear war between the United States and the Soviet Union. Their existence makes conventional combat or even serious diplomatic confrontation between the superpowers less likely than would otherwise be the case because they make the risk of escalation to the holocaust greater. (To a very substantial degree the British and French nuclear capabilities undoubtedly play the same role.) Some argue that tactical nuclear weapons are justified because they obviate the need for large expenditures on conventional forces and inhibit conventional conflict. However others, the author included, argue that the fire break between conventional war and an all-out thermonuclear exchange should be broadened as much as possible so that if conventional war does break out a nuclear holocaust will be less likely. They argue that to the extent that either superpower and its allies are concerned about a conventional attack somewhere within its sphere of interest, they should rely on deterring or meeting it with conventional strength rather than relying on the fear of nuclear escalation as a deterrent.

In contrast to the case of superpower strategic nuclear capabilities, there is no consensus regarding the objectives that tactical capabilities should serve. Therefore, in attempting to control them there would be great domestic political difficulties in the United States and probably other countries, and also serious intra-alliance problems.

Even in the unlikely event that domestic and international consensus could be reached regarding desired tactical nuclear force postures, there would be no serious near-term prospect of negotiating limitations affecting them. This is because there are no means to verify any agreement short of very intrusive and, for the present, non-negotiable inspection arrangements. The nuclear weapons themselves cannot be monitored by unilateral intelligence techniques and virtually all of the delivery systems are dual purpose: they can also deliver non-nuclear ordnance. And clearly we are a long way from negotiating any arms control agreements that will have a major impact on conventional forces.

Finally, there is one other reason for not linking the tactical to the strategic nuclear problem. The primary interest of the smaller nuclear powers—and would-be nuclear powers—has been in nuclear weapons regarded as strategic. To the best of the author's knowledge, Sweden is the only nation that has seriously considered developing nuclear weapons primarily for tactical purposes, and even there the issue is apparently no longer active.

Since the preparation of this chapter, the United States has continued with its MIRV test programs and has actually begun the deployment of the Minuteman III missile with MIRV's. The deployment decision could still be reversed as a result of a SALT agreement, but that seems more difficult and far less likely to achieve than it did in early 1970.

3   Horizontal Proliferation of Nuclear Weapons

George Bunn

This chapter will discuss the scope and future impact of Articles I and II of the Non-Proliferation Treaty on the potential spread of nuclear weapons to countries that do not now have these weapons. This spread is sometimes referred to as "horizontal proliferation."

Parties to the Treaty

Some idea of the number of parties the treaty is likely to have is essential to determine the impact it will have on horizontal proliferation. When the treaty went into force on March 5, 1970, ninety-seven countries had then signed.[1] Signature without formal ratification does not create a full-fledged treaty obligation. But it does indicate an intention to become a party and it does require the signing country to refrain from any act that would defeat the object of the treaty until that country has made up its mind on formal ratification. By March 5, 1970, the day the treaty came into force, forty-nine countries had made up their minds and deposited their formal instruments of ratification.[2]

Only a very few countries with the ability and incentive to get the bomb in the next two decades have failed to sign. Of the seven non-nuclear countries generally considered to have industrial economies probably capable of supporting the manufacture of a sizable number of reasonably sophisticated nuclear weapons and of systems for their delivery within five to ten years,[3] six have signed the treaty: Australia, Canada (which also has ratified), Italy, Japan, Sweden (which also has ratified), and West Germany. Of this group of seven, only India has indicated an intention not to sign.

India has the capability and could have the incentive to become a nuclear weapon power during the 1970's. She has said, however, that she would not do so. Her case is discussed in more detail later.

If one considers the countries that might produce nuclear weapons of less sophistication, or with less delivery capability, but within the next ten to twenty years, the list of countries, of course, grows longer. Such a list would probably include Argentina, Austria, Belgium, Brazil, Chile, Czechoslovakia, Hungary, Israel, the Netherlands, Pakistan, Poland, South Africa, Spain, Switzerland, the United Arab Republic, and Yugoslavia.[4] Nine of these sixteen have already signed the treaty.[5] Three others have signed the Latin American Nuclear Free Zone Treaty, which would present a serious obstacle to their acquisition of nuclear weapons.[6]

Of the remainder, only Israel has the likely capability and possible incentive to acquire nuclear weapons and an effective delivery capability within this decade. Israel has said, however, that she would not be the first to introduce nuclear weapons into the Middle East.

It is unclear what combination of incentives and threats would be likely to deter the acquisition of nuclear weapons by India or Israel. Certainly the negotiation of a treaty banning all nuclear weapon tests, underground as well as elsewhere, would be a forward step in the arms-control field. Both countries have supported such a treaty in the past. Either or both might be prepared to become parties to a comprehensive test-ban treaty, even if they do not become parties to the Non-Proliferation Treaty, because a comprehensive test ban would prohibit nuclear weapon testing by nuclear powers as well as by non-nuclear powers. India particularly has complained of the "discrimination" inherent in the Non-Proliferation Treaty in that it limits the nuclear ambitions only of the non-nuclear powers. Other factors—for example, threats to national security which nuclear weapons might deter and the enhanced prestige that seems to many to accompany their acquisition—will no doubt play important parts in the ultimate decision of each country. What might happen to the treaty if either India or Israel went nuclear is discussed below.

Two nuclear powers have said they would not join the treaty: China and France. How the interests of either would be served by giving nuclear weapons, or the information necessary to make them, to non-nuclear weapon countries is unclear. France, indeed, has said she "will behave in the future in this field exactly as the states adhering to the treaty."[7] In any event, most potential recipients of weapons or assistance from China or France will be obligated by their own adherence to the treaty not to receive nuclear weapons or assistance in their manufacture.

Scope of Articles I and II

This section and the next are written on the assumption that *observance* of Articles I and II of the treaty will be universal or nearly so even though some important countries may not become parties. What may happen if this assumption turns out to be wrong is discussed in the last section.

Article I deals with the obligation of nuclear powers.[8] First, they cannot "transfer" nuclear weapons or "control" over nuclear weapons "to any recipient whatsoever." This means that nuclear powers cannot give up physical custody of their nuclear weapons, or provide sufficient access to their weapons so that they can be taken away, or set off, by anyone else. Nor can the nuclear powers give up their power to make the final decision on the firing of their weapons.

Second, nuclear powers cannot assist non-nuclear states to "manufacture or otherwise acquire" nuclear weapons. "Manufacture" of nuclear weapons would clearly include the construction of an experimental or prototype nuclear explosive device, or of components that could have relevance only to such a device.[9] It would clearly not include the production of fissionable material or the construction of a reactor in a peaceful program under the safeguards required by other articles of the treaty.[10]

Third, the prohibitions in Article I apply not only to nuclear weapons, but also to "other nuclear explosive devices." Nuclear explosive devices developed for peaceful purposes are treated like nuclear weapons because such devices could be used as weapons and the technology for making them is essentially indistinguishable from that of weapons. As a United Kingdom representative said, a device which could move "a million tons of earth to dig a canal . . . could just as easily pulverize a city of a million people."[11]

Article II deals with the obligations of non-nuclear states and is almost the mirror reflection of Article I. First, such states cannot receive the "transfer" of nuclear weapons, or control over them, from any "transfer or transferor whatsoever." Second, and probably more important, they cannot "manufacture or otherwise acquire" nuclear weapons, or seek or receive assistance for such manufacture. "Manufacture" would, of course, include the same kinds of conduct in Article II as in Article I. Third, as in Article I, these prohibitions are applicable not only to nuclear weapons, but also to "other nuclear explosive devices."

Impact of Articles I and II in Particular Situations

A number of questions on the future impact of Articles I and II will arise even if observance of these articles is universal, or nearly so. Some of these questions are as follows:

1. Will the treaty interfere with present arrangements within NATO for the defense of the United States and its allies against nuclear attack?

No. The 1965 Soviet draft non-proliferation treaty appeared to prohibit existing arrangements for the deployment in allied territory by the United States of its nuclear weapons under its custody and control, for the training of allied troops for defense against nuclear attack, and for allied consultations and planning for such defense. The United States representatives made it clear that no treaty was possible if the Soviets intended to change these arrangements. The compromise agreed upon would not.[12]

An interpretation of the treaty, worked out by the United States with its NATO allies and given to the Soviets, states that Articles I and II do "not deal with arrangements for deployment of nuclear weapons within allied territory as these do not involve any transfer of nuclear weapons or control over them unless and until a decision were made to go to war, at which time the treaty would no longer be controlling."[13] This interpretation would not, of course, preclude substitution of new nuclear weapons for those the United States now has deployed on allied territory, provided, of course, that the United States retained custody and control of the new weapons.

The interpretation also states that Articles I and II do "not deal with allied consultations and planning on nuclear defense so long as no transfer of nuclear weapons or control over them results." Thus, the current consultations and planning of the seven-nation NATO Nuclear Planning Group to develop political guidelines for the possible use of tactical nuclear weapons in Europe are not prohibited by the treaty. These guidelines recognize that while "great weight" would be given to the views of the allies most vitally concerned, the final decision on use of nuclear weapons would be made by the United States President.[14]

2. Would Articles I and II prohibit transfer of nuclear weapons, or control over them, to a multilateral force (MLF) of sea-going surface vessels owned and controlled (by majority vote) by a group or alliance of countries including the United States?

Yes. Articles I and II prohibit transfers to "any recipient whatsoever." The MLF project was a major obstacle to negotiating the treaty for several years. Not until after the MLF had clearly and publicly failed did serious talks begin. While the United States was to retain custody and control of the nuclear weapons in the initial stages of the last plan discussed, the U.S. proposal for evolution of the MLF did leave the door open for eventual European control.[15] The NATO interpretation, referred to earlier, states that Articles I and II would "bar transfer of nuclear weapons (including ownership) or control over them to any recipient, including a multilateral entity."

The treaty would not preclude a new United States of Europe from acquiring nuclear weapons by inheriting the weapons of one of its constituents. If, for example, the six Common Market countries joined together in a new, unified state, the new state would be a nuclear state because France, one of its constituents, had been. The NATO interpretation makes clear that Articles I and II do "not deal with the problem of European unity, and would not bar succession by a new federated European state to the nuclear status of one of its former components. A new federated European state would have to control all of its external security functions including defense and foreign policy matters relating to external security, but would not have to be so centralized as to assume all governmental functions."

3. Would the treaty permit the transfer of antiballistic missiles with nuclear warheads to NATO control?

No. The treaty would prohibit the transfer of "nuclear weapons" or control over them to "any recipient whatsoever." This would, of course, include the transfer of nuclear warheads for antiballistic missiles, or control over them, to NATO. Since defensive weapons can be used offensively, or can be used to make offensive weapons, no other result would be consistent with the objectives of the treaty.[16] The treaty would not, however, prohibit a U.S. antiballistic missile system designed to protect NATO allies and deployed on their territory but under United States custody and control, if effective command and control arrangements could be worked out given the very short response time involved.

4. Would the treaty prohibit the transfer of nuclear delivery vehicles such as Polaris submarines or missiles to NATO or to NATO allies?

No, provided that no transfer of nuclear weapons resulted. Articles I and II prohibit the transfer of "nuclear weapons or other nuclear explosive devices." These do not include delivery vehicles such as submarines, missiles, or aircraft.[17] The NATO interpretation, referred to earlier, states that the treaty "does not deal with and therefore does not prohibit, transfer of nuclear delivery vehicles or delivery systems, or control over them to any recipient, so long as such transfer does not involve bombs or warheads."

The United States has in fact sold American aircraft designed to carry nuclear weapons to some of its NATO allies. But the United States maintains custody and control of the nuclear weapons that would be used by these aircraft in the event that war broke out and the President gave an order to use the weapons. As President Johnson put it: "The release of nuclear weapons would come by Presidential decision alone. Complex codes and electronic devices prevent any unauthorized action . . . . An elaborate system of checks and counterchecks, procedural and mechanical, guard against any unauthorized nuclear bursts. In addition, since 1961, we have placed permissive-action links on several of our weapons. These are electro-mechanical locks which must be opened by secret combination before action at all is possible . . . . "[18]

5. Would Articles I and II prohibit a United States ally on whose territory U.S. nuclear weapons were deployed from having a veto over the use of those nuclear weapons?

No. Under Articles I and II, such an ally could not acquire "control" of United States nuclear weapons. But a veto on the firing of nuclear weapons from one's own territory is not the affirmative and final decision-making power which constitutes control for the purposes of Articles I and II. The United States has taken the view that an ally could insist on a veto on the use of nuclear weapons on its territory without violating the treaty.[19]

Possible Causes of Breakdown

1. If the United States and the Soviet Union show no restraint in limiting their own nuclear arms race, major non-nuclear "threshold" powers may withdraw from the treaty in five years or more. If this happened, the treaty might have little reason for continued existence.

For many non-nuclear countries, the obligation the treaty imposes on the United States and the Soviet Union to "pursue negotiations in good faith on effective measures relating to the cessation of the nuclear arms race . . . " is a major *quid pro quo* for adherence to the treaty. If there is continued nuclear stockpiling by nuclear powers and observance of the treaty by non-nuclear powers, these non-nuclear countries see the strong getting stronger and the weak getting weaker. Perhaps the primary reason they insisted upon a review conference within five years after the treaty went into force was to keep the pressure on the United States and the Soviet Union to achieve agreement. They have been watching the hesitant approach of these two countries toward the Strategic Arms Limitation Talks (SALT) in Vienna with immense interest. If no real progress has been made in five years, many non-nuclear powers may attempt to use the review conference to lay the basis for their later withdrawal from the treaty. If enough countries join in this effort and then withdraw, the treaty structure would probably collapse.

2. In the event India or Israel acquire nuclear weapons, the entire treaty system could fail.

India faces a hostile, nuclear-armed China that attacked her with conventional weapons in 1962. India has refused to join the treaty and has the capacity, at great sacrifice to other objectives, to acquire nuclear weapons and the essentials of a delivery system within this decade. While she has said she would not acquire nuclear weapons, she has not forsworn development of nuclear explosive devices for peaceful purposes such as building canals, harbors, and dams. Such devices can also be used for bombs.

Whether India's incentives and capabilities will be sufficient to produce a nuclear weapon capability in the next decade is unclear. But should she do so, the repercussions could be great. Pakistan could be expected to pursue the same path, or at least to seek a nuclear guarantee from China. Japan might feel that a military alliance with the United States was not sufficient to protect her security vis-à-vis China, or her prestige as a major power in Asia, if India had chosen the nuclear route. Australia might not wish to be far behind India or Japan.

A similar chain reaction might well follow the acquisition of nuclear weapons by Israel—which may also have both the capability and the incentive. The UAR, which has the incentive but not the capability, would no doubt seek nuclear assistance or a guarantee from its protector, the Soviet Union. This might well lead to the deployment in the UAR of Soviet nuclear weapons under the control of Soviet troops. What would the U.S. response be then?

If either India or Israel acquires nuclear weapons, West Germany's NATO allies may possibly have a hard time persuading her not to follow suit. She is the target for over 500 nuclear-tipped Soviet missiles and a great deal of Soviet hostility. Some twenty Soviet divisions face her in East Germany. If allied troops are substantially reduced in West Germany, the West Germans will be relying increasingly on U.S. tactical nuclear weapons deployed in Germany as a defense against conventional attack by Soviet troops.[20] These weapons cannot be used without an order from the U.S. President, who by giving that order would risk a Soviet nuclear attack on the United States. United States participation in the North Atlantic Treaty is now subject to termination on one year's notice—an insufficient period for Germany to acquire a nuclear capability of its own.

While the immediate future will not see United States withdrawal from NATO, the distant future is harder for Germany to predict. As we shall see, the eventual disintegration of NATO itself must be considered as at least possible. At the moment, Germany does not have ambitions for nuclear weapons. But acquisition of nuclear weapons by India or Israel combined with a new Berlin crisis or a similar situation could bring to power in Germany a government dedicated to nuclear weapon goals. If Germany did in fact achieve a nuclear capability, the anti-proliferation system established by the treaty would quite likely collapse.

3. If NATO came to an end as an effective military alliance, its fall could also bring down the Non-Proliferation Treaty.

Since August, 1969, any party to the North Atlantic Treaty has had the right to end its own obligations upon one year's notice. Major non-nuclear European allies of the United States, particularly West Germany, rely upon NATO for their nuclear deterrent against possible Soviet attack by conventional or nuclear arms. Should enough countries withdraw from NATO to bring it to an end as an effective alliance, or should the United States alone withdraw, West Germany, then Italy, and then some of the smaller countries might well look to their own nuclear defenses. Germany's concern on this score was such that the United States felt the need to reassure her that if NATO were to dissolve, this fact might be taken by non-nuclear NATO members as affecting their supreme national interests and therefore justifying their withdrawal from the Non-Proliferation Treaty.[21]

This and the two preceding hypothetical situations have been concerned in large part with actions that "threshold" powers might take in light of perceived threats to their national security primarily from *conventional* attack. The next two hypothetical situations involve the threat or occurrence of *nuclear* attack.

4. If aggression with nuclear weapons against a non-nuclear party to the treaty occurs without an effective response by the United Nations Security Council or by a nuclear power, the aggression could bring down the treaty structure.

A *quid pro quo* to many non-aligned non-nuclear countries for joining the treaty was the declaration made by the three nuclear proponents of the Treaty with respect to assistance to them in the event they were threatened by nuclear aggression. The United Kingdom, the United States, and the Soviet Union each declared that aggression with nuclear weapons against a non-nuclear power—or the threat of such aggression—would "create a qualitatively new situation in which the nuclear-weapon states which are permanent members of the United National Security Council would have to act immediately through the Security Council to take the measures necessary to counter such aggression or to remove the threat of aggression. . . ." Each of the three nuclear powers affirmed its intention, as a permanent member of the United Nations Security Council, "to seek immediate Security Council action to provide assistance, in accordance with the Charter, to any non-nuclear-weapon State party to the treaty on the nonproliferation of nuclear weapons that is a victim of an act of aggression or an object of a threat of aggression in which nuclear weapons are used." Each of the three also reaffirmed the inherent right of *collective* self-defense against attack, "including nuclear attack," "until the Security Council has taken measures necessary to maintain international peace and security."[22] They thus implied that collective defense against a nuclear attack upon a non-nuclear party to the treaty could be available even if the Security Council failed to act.

If aggression with nuclear weapons against a non-nuclear treaty party were to occur without effective response, other non-nuclear parties might well decide that a fundamental basis for their adherence to the treaty had been removed and that they should therefore withdraw from the treaty. While the Security Council resolution itself may not have been the basis for much reliance, it articulated an assumption that underlies the treaty: In a world in which nuclear aggression can be successful against those who have forsworn nuclear weapons, no treaty can halt nuclear spread. Successful nuclear aggression against a non-nuclear party to the treaty would certainly justify withdrawal by other non-nuclear parties that were threatened. Enough such withdrawals would bring down the treaty.

5. In the event of general war involving the nuclear powers, the treaty would no longer be controlling in the area of combat.

The United States nuclear defense arrangements with its NATO allies generally provide, among other things, that in the event the United States President gives an order in time of war authorizing the use of nuclear weapons deployed in Europe at the military bases of our allies, the weapons covered by the order become subject to the military command of NATO and can be turned over to allied forces for use. It is for this reason that the NATO interpretation of the treaty, referred to earlier, states that the treaty "does not deal with arrangements for deployment of nuclear weapons within allied territory as they do not involve any transfer of nuclear weapons or control over them *unless and until a decision is made to go to war, at which time the Treaty would no longer be controlling*" (emphasis added). This language has been construed by the United States as applying in the case "of general war involving the nuclear powers" but not in the case of a "limited, local conflict not involving a nuclear-weapon state."[23]

If nuclear weapons were given to the armed forces of United States or Soviet allies in Europe during a general war involving the nuclear powers, a central purpose of the treaty would have failed even if no nuclear weapons were used. Not only would the treaty not be controlling in the area of battle, but non-nuclear countries outside that area might well exercise their withdrawal rights. And if nuclear weapons were used, the entire treaty structure would probably collapse.

Conclusion

These are some of the potential situations in which the treaty may have an impact on future nuclear developments, or may break down if particular events come to pass. If the treaty is a success, it will be because the two nuclear powers that largely authored it—the Soviet Union and the United States—have been able to cooperate successfully in maintaining the peace, in exercising restraint over their own nuclear ambitions, and in keeping the lid on those of others. If cooperation in these matters breaks down seriously, whether in the Middle East or in the SALT negotiations, the chances for long-term success of the Non-Proliferation Treaty will be greatly reduced.

Part 2   Atoms for Peace

4 Military Potential of Civilian Nuclear Power

Victor Gilinsky

Introduction

The inclusion in the Non-Proliferation Treaty of an article providing for safeguards on peaceful nuclear facilities in non-nuclear weapon countries reflects a concern that future nuclear weapons programs may be initiated with fissile material—in practice, plutonium and uranium-235—diverted from civilian nuclear power programs. There is little question that by the end of this decade civilian nuclear power programs may provide many non-nuclear weapon countries with plutonium stockpiles. A few non-nuclear countries will also have production capacity for highly enriched uranium—that is, uranium that is almost pure uranium-235.

The availability of fissile materials is especially critical for, despite the difficulties of nuclear weapon design and fabrication, the acquisition of fissile materials in suitable amounts and of suitable quality is probably the chief technical obstacle to the initial production of nuclear weapons. As a result, plutonium or uranium-235 production rates are often taken as a very rough indication of a country's technical capacity to produce simple nuclear warheads. Detailed country-by-country estimates of plutonium production can be derived from projections of the installed nuclear electrical generating capacity for the countries concerned (see Table 1). Of course, the estimates are only as accurate in detail as the nuclear power projections on which they are based, but taken together they clearly indicate that within a decade the yearly production rate of plutonium in many non-nuclear countries will be large with respect to the requirements for tens and, in some cases, hundreds of warheads.

41

TABLE 1

Rough Projections of Plutonium Production Capacities
in Selected Non-Nuclear Weapon States

Country	Estimated installed nuclear capacity (Mwe)		Estimated plutonium production capacity (kg per year)[a]	
	1975	1980	1975	1980
FRG	5,000-	20,000	1,000-	4,000
Japan	5,000-	20,000	1,000-	4,000
Canada	2,500-	6,000	600-	1,500
Sweden	2,500-	4,000	500-	800
Italy	1,400-	5,000	300-	1,000
Spain	2,000-	5,000	400-	1,000
Switzerland	1,000-	3,000	200-	600
India	1,200-	2,000	300-	500
Argentina	300-	1,000	100-	300
Israel	—		10-	
Other	5,000-	15,000	1,000-	3,000
Rounded total for non-nuclear countries	26,000-	81,000	5,000-17,000	
United States (for comparison)	50,000-120,000		10,000-25,000	

[a]Additional time must be allowed for extraction of plutonium.

Our purpose here is to look behind these numbers. In order to assess risks more accurately, and especially to make informed choices among alternative safeguard measures, it is helpful to obtain some idea of the principal relevant technical factors. Not surprisingly, some forms of plutonium, and some kinds of civilian nuclear facilities, lend themselves more easily to military purposes than others. Of course, the availability for military purposes of civilian nuclear materials depends ultimately on political decisions. It is certainly not meant to suggest here that what is technically possible could easily occur, but it is useful to know the limits within which political decisions can be made.

In this spirit, the following is intended as a short primer, for the policy-oriented non-technical reader, on the military potential of the civilian nuclear fuel cycle—that is, its capacity to supply fissile material useful for weapons—in the absence of safeguards. In passing, it should be emphasized that apart from the similarity of the materials involved and the means of their production, nuclear explosive technology and nuclear power technology have almost nothing in common. Although this is perhaps an obvious point, one often finds the word "nuclear" used loosely.

Fissile Materials

Nuclear Weapons

The precise amount of fissile material required for a warhead (a "critical mass") naturally depends on the design. For illustrative purposes, we shall arbitrarily use 5 kg of plutonium and 20 kg of uranium-235 as nominal warhead equivalents,[1] but our general conclusions are not sensitive to the precise figures.

To create a nuclear explosion—a very fast chain fission reaction—it is necessary rapidly to assemble the critical mass of plutonium or uranium-235 and to initiate the reaction at the right moment. The assembly may be performed by compressing a single subcritical[2] spherical mass, as in the so-called implosion-type devices, or, in the case of uranium-235, by simply bringing together two subcritical masses, as in the so-called gun-type devices (such as the bomb dropped on Hiroshima). Gun-type weapons make less economic use of precious fissile material, but they are easier to design.

Note, however, that a plutonium gun-type weapon will not work. If two subcritical masses of plutonium are brought together in a gun-type device, spontaneous neutrons from the ever-present contaminant plutonium-240 would set off a premature chain reaction ("predetonation"), which would blow the masses apart before an appreciable amount of energy was released. Even the plutonium implosion-type devices, which assemble the plutonium much faster, can be severely limited in performance—the stray neutrons introduce a random reduction in the energy of the explosion—if excessive amounts of plutonium-240 are present, as is usually the case with plutonium produced in civilian reactors. Therefore, the military usefulness of a particular quantity of plutonium depends to some degree on the method of production.

Plutonium

Because uranium-235 is the only naturally occurring material that will support a chain fission reaction, it is the necessary starting point for all applications of nuclear energy, civilian and military. Natural uranium, of which less than 1 percent is uranium-235 (the rest is more or less inert uranium-238) will not alone support a chain fission reaction because of excessive neutron capture in uranium-238. But if mixed with a moderator—a material that slows down neutrons—such as heavy water or graphite, a large enough quantity of natural uranium can be made to sustain a slow chain reaction. This is the principle of the nuclear reactor.

Uranium-238 is not just a nuisance, however, because after capturing a neutron, a uranium-238 nucleus is converted into a plutonium nucleus (more precisely, a plutonium-239 nucleus—that is, the plutonium isotope of atomic weight 239). This is the basis of plutonium production. The uranium fuel is removed periodically and the plutonium is separated out by chemical methods (see Figure 1).

FIGURE 1

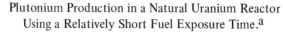

Plutonium Production in a Natural Uranium Reactor
Using a Relatively Short Fuel Exposure Time.[a]

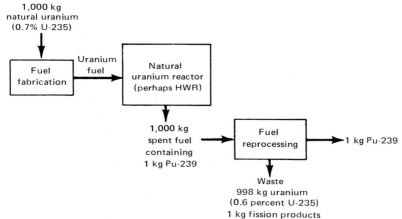

[a]The numbers are only approximately correct. We have also neglected material losses.

In military production reactors, the concentration of the contaminant plutonium-240 in the fuel rods is kept down to less than a few percent by fairly rapid fuel replacement so that each rod is subjected to a fairly small irradiation before it is reprocessed. Note that the plutonium-240 is a by-product formed from plutonium-239 just as the plutonium-239 was formed in the first place from uranium-238.

To produce the highly enriched uranium needed for nuclear explosions, the natural uranium must be processed in enrichment facilities, sometimes called isotope separation facilities. The uranium-235 is concentrated in a small part of the original material by depleting the larger part, which is then discarded (see Figure 2). So far only the gaseous diffusion method has been used on a large scale. In this method, separation is effected by passing a gaseous uranium compound (uranium hexafluoride) through porous barriers. The lighter uranium-235 component passes through slightly faster. This process is then repeated several thousand times. Economic uranium enrichment by gaseous diffusion requires a considerable industrial undertaking, and much of the technology is secret and tightly held. Such facilities exist only in the nuclear weapon states—in the United States (Oak Ridge, Paducah, and Portsmouth), the Soviet Union (location not divulged), United Kingdom (Capenhurst), France (Pierrelatte), and China (Lanchow).

FIGURE 2

Sample Feed, Product, and Waste in Uranium Enrichment for Weapons[a]

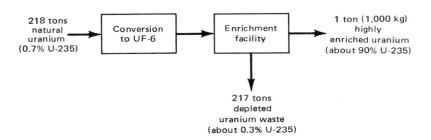

[a]If the figures represent yearly inputs and outputs, then the enrichment facility would have a capacity approximately 1 percent of total U.S. enrichment capacity.

An alternative method of uranium enrichment is the gas centrifuge method now under development in a number of countries. Here the gaseous compound of uranium is passed through a cascade of rapidly spinning cylinders— gas centrifuges. Loosely speaking, the heavier (uranium-238) component tends to be selectively pushed toward the cylinder wall. This method lends itself more easily to small-scale applications.

Civilian Nuclear Fuel Cycle
The nuclear fuel cycle for a nuclear power reactor fueled with natural uranium involves essentially the same facilities as those for a military plutoni-

um production reactor (see Figure 1). Of course, the mode of operation is different in the two cases because the civilian reactor is operated to produce steam economically in order to power a turbine generator—a power reactor is, in fact, just another device to make steam.

More economical than natural uranium reactors are those that use slightly enriched uranium fuel, about 2 to 4 percent uranium-235 (see Figure 3). The U.S. and Soviet civilian nuclear power programs are based on such reactors and probably most of the reactors to be installed elsewhere over the next decade will also be of this type. The French have now officially confirmed[3] that they will switch from natural uranium reactors to the U.S.-type light water reactors that use slightly enriched fuel elements and ordinary water as a coolant and moderator. The British earlier gave up their line of gas-cooled natural uranium reactors for advanced gas-cooled reactors, which also use slightly enriched fuel. This leaves the Canadian heavy water reactors as the only important national line of natural uranium reactor. In the future, for economic reasons, even these may be used with very slightly enriched fuel.

Plutonium Production in Civilian Power Reactors

Generally speaking, the diversion of plutonium produced in civilian reactors is the chief danger associated with civilian nuclear power programs. While the future availability in presently non-nuclear weapons countries of highly enriched uranium is still uncertain, the rate of reactor installation in these countries makes it fairly certain that large amounts of plutonium will be available.

The rate of plutonium production depends on the type of reactor and the mode of operation, but, in any case, substantial production of plutonium is an unavoidable by-product of the operation of uranium-fueled power reactors. Under normal commercial operating conditions, light water reactors produce about 200-300 kg per year of plutonium, or about 50 warhead equivalents, for every 1,000 Mwe (megawatts of electric generating capacity)—a capacity required by a city of about a million people. Natural uranium power reactors typically produce plutonium at about twice this rate.

The civilian plutonium, after it is chemically separated, can be used as fuel in present-day reactors or it can be stored for future use in advanced plutonium-fueled reactors such as "fast breeders." Our concern is that it could also be diverted to military use.

However, because fuel is usually kept in a power reactor for a relatively long time, the plutonium normally produced in these reactors contains significant amounts of the isotope plutonium-240. Typical plutonium-240 content in commerical plutonium is expected to be about 30 percent, compared with the usual limit of no more than a few percent plutonium-240 in plutonium

FIGURE 3

Example of a Civilian Nuclear Fuel Cycle for Reactors Fueled with Slightly Enriched Uranium.[a]

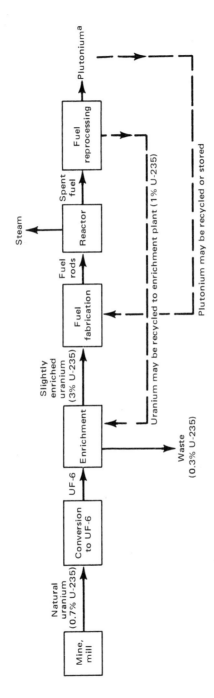

[a]The plutonium could be recycled in the reactor or stockpiled for future use in a following generation of fast breeder reactors.

47

meant for military use. Since for practical purposes the plutonium-240 cannot be removed, civilian plutonium is generally not suitable for simple, predictable, efficient weapons. Whether a country might be willing to initiate a military program with unpredictable or inferior weapons cannot be easily prejudged. However, it is clearly necessary to keep this limitation in mind when drawing conclusions about the military usefulness of a particular stockpile of plutonium.

Of course, civilian reactors can also be operated to produce plutonium with a fairly low plutonium-240 content by replacing the fuel rods more frequently. This is easy with most natural uranium reactors, for they are generally designed to be refueled "on-line," without shutting down the reactor. But light water reactors, which will account for most of the world's civilian nuclear power capacity for the next two decades, have to be shut down for weeks each time the fuel rods are replaced. These reactors, therefore, do not lend themselves easily to the production of plutonium for military purposes: power production is disrupted, the change in mode of operation is more difficult to conceal, and the plutonium production rate is lower.

Let us now turn to the rest of the nuclear fuel cycle.

Fuel Reprocessing and Fuel Fabrication

Used nuclear fuel is highly radioactive and cannot be easily handled. To extract its plutonium, the fuel must be treated in special reprocessing facilities. With present technology it generally takes at least a year from the time the radioactive fuel rods are withdrawn from a reactor to the time the plutonium is available for fabrication into new fuel elements. Clearly, a country must have a fuel reprocessing facility before it can have independent access to plutonium produced in its reactors.

Small reprocessing facilities are not economical, but this technology is easier to acquire than uranium enrichment technology. A number of nonnuclear countries already have constructed facilities, perhaps to obtain industrial experience, and others will soon   have them.

It needs to be stressed, however, that any considerable speed-up of the normal refueling schedule in order to limit the plutonium-240 content of the fuel rods implies a need for substantial excess reprocessing and fuel-fabrication capacity. For example, if the refueling schedule is speeded up by a factor of five to reduce plutonium-240 content to a few percent, then about a five-fold increase in reprocessing and fabrication capacity will be required. Since it would be unusual for a country to have a large amount of excess capacity in reprocessing and fabrication, it would generally not be possible to speed up refueling on a large fraction of   reactor capacity.

Naturally, a time will come—perhaps after 1980—when the amounts of fissile materials available in the civilian economy, especially plutonium, will be so large as to dwarf reasonable military needs. At that time, the possible demands caused by a nuclear weapon program based on fissile material from the civilian economy will be relatively smaller and more easily satisfied. Until then, it will be easy to divert enough plutonium from the civilian economy to build inferior and uncertain weapons, but much less easy to provide oneself with a sizable stockpile of efficient, predictable weapons.

In passing, we should note that the commercial importance of plutonium derives mainly from the fact that nuclear industries in advanced countries are planning for eventual reliance on plutonium-fueled fast breeder reactors, reactors that produce, or "breed," more fissile plutonium than they consume in the generation of power. Almost all the civilian plutonium produced in the next few years, thousands of kilograms, will be used in fast breeder research and development efforts.

Uranium Enrichment

As we have indicated earlier, most nuclear power reactors use fuel that contains slightly enriched uranium—2 to 4 percent uranium-235. It does not now appear that highly enriched uranium will be commonly used in civilian nuclear programs. (We shall later mention a possible exception.) But there is the possibility that enrichment technology in the hands of non-nuclear countries will lead to the construction of facilities for the production of highly enriched uranium. This accounts, in part, for the considerable efforts the U.S. Atomic Energy Commission has made to keep U.S. enrichment technology secret and to discourage foreign enrichment efforts.

There are, in fact, efforts under way in a number of industrial non-nuclear weapon countries (especially the Federal Republic of Germany, the Netherlands, and Japan) to develop domestic enrichment technology, particularly gas centrifuge technology, which is the main alternative to gaseous diffusion. There are strong indications, for example the recent U.K.-Netherlands-F.R.G. agreement,[4] that at least some of these ventures will lead to the construction of commerical uranium enrichment facilities in non-nuclear countries. These would provide alternative sources of slightly enriched uranium and would thereby reduce the leverage the United States has enjoyed over foreign nuclear power programs because of its effective monopoly on commercial enrichment services. But more importantly, because the economics of gas centrifuge enrichment plants would be relatively independent of enrichment plant size (as opposed to great economies of scale in gaseous diffusion plants), successful development of centrifuge technology could lead to the existence of relatively small national enrichment plants in many countries.[5]

Although commercial gas centrifuge enrichment plants would probably be designed to produce slightly enriched uranium—more accurately called low enrichment uranium—they could be modified, or at least easily enlarged to produce highly enriched uranium. To enrich a yearly supply of fuel for a 1,000 Mwe light water reactor requires an enrichment plant (or an equivalent share of a larger plant) somewhat smaller than the one illustrated[6] (see Figure 2.) If modified to produce highly enriched uranium, it could produce each year over 500 kg of 90 percent uranium-235, or over 25 warhead equivalents. Gaseous diffusion plants are probably less easy to modify, but they could be augmented with small gas centrifuge plants to achieve the same purpose.

It is important to note that it is much easier to extract highly enriched uranium from low enrichment uranium than from natural uranium. An enrichment facility of given capacity can produce highly enriched uranium several times more rapidly if fed with low enrichment uranium than if it were supplied with natural uranium. This means that stocks of low enrichment uranium could be upgraded rapidly by relatively small enrichment plants. Therefore, while low enrichment uranium cannot itself be used as a nuclear explosive, it is not a material of negligible military significance, at least where enrichment technology is potentially available.

The continued growth of nuclear power programs based on U.S. or Soviet-type light water reactors and U.K.-type advanced gas-cooled reactors ensures that slightly enriched uranium will become a common commercial commodity. Conceivably, in the future large stockpiles may exist in a number of non-nuclear countries. To counter criticism over "security of supply," and to discourage foreign enrichment efforts, the U.S. Atomic Energy Commission has agreed to permit nations to stockpile up to a five-year forward supply. Stockpiling may also take place for other reasons. For example, the Federal Republic of Germany has agreed to stockpile a large quantity of slightly enriched uranium as part of an agreement to offset the cost of U.S. troops in Germany.[7]

Finally, it needs to be mentioned that *highly* enriched uranium could still become an important commercial nuclear material. High-temperature gas-cooled reactors are designed to use as fuel over 90 percent enriched uranium-235. If reactors of this type became commercially competitive, commercial gas centrifuge plants may be built specifically to produce highly enriched uranium.

Diversion Options

The most straightforward way to acquire fissile material for weapons is, of course, by an open military production program. But it takes several years to construct facilities for producing fissile material, and then another year or two before appreciable quantities of material are available for weapons. In short, fissile material is the long lead-time item in a beginning nuclear weapons program. The principal significance of a civilian nuclear program in this context is that it offers an immediate source of fissile material that can be used to reduce this lead time, generally also at a considerable reduction in cost. (This did not apply to the existing nuclear weapon powers because in the past civilian programs were very small.)

Shortening the time it takes to acquire nuclear weapons, made possible by diversion, reduces the risks involved. The time between the first clear external evidence of a nuclear weapons program and development of a strategically significant force could be one of special vulnerability. For this reason, it may become attractive to divert materials and facilities from the civilian nuclear economy. In addition, the attractiveness of various diversion options may depend strongly on the times they take to execute.

The same reasoning, of course, leads to the suggestion of clandestine diversion in order to delay warning and therefore further reduce the possibility of foreign reactions intended to inhibit the military program in question. Conversely, the role of safeguards is to provide reliable early warning of diversion in order to permit at least the possibility of effective response.

There are several ways in which warning might be delayed. Most discussions and analyses have focused on the diversion by a non-nuclear state of fissile material from its own civilian nuclear program at a low rate—below some detection threshold—over a period of time sufficiently long to assemble a desired weapons stockpile. The limits on the probabilities of maintaining secrecy would, however, severely restrict the size of the force that could be assembled in this manner. Moreover, such an approach might delay warning, but it would also delay the completion of the weapons acquisition process. Another possible course, at the other extreme, would be a large diversion, one that is bound to be discovered in time but which could perhaps be kept secret during the initial period of rapid warhead fabrication. Preparatory warhead development and design could probably be kept secret since these would be relatively small efforts, and could probably be conducted free of safeguards and without violation of the Non-Proliferation Treaty.[8]

It is often asked how countries interested in an option to produce nuclear weapons would organize their civilian programs. In a limited sense, many countries have, and many more will have, an option to manufacture nuclear weapons. It is largely a question of time. Clearly, countries interested in a relatively short-range option to build nuclear weapons can be expected to move toward sizable self-contained nuclear power programs that can be used to rapidly supply fissile material of suitable quality to a military program. In itself, however, this does not prescribe a specific course of action. Generally speaking, in less developed countries (those that cannot aspire to domestic enrichment facilities) opening the nuclear weapons option would mean building natural uranium reactors for plutonium production and domestic reprocessing and possibly fuel fabrication facilities. More advanced non-nuclear countries might also seek to develop uranium enrichment technology, particularly gas centrifuge technology.

When available, uranium-235 is particularly suitable for rapid production of simple nuclear weapons. It requires no reprocessing delay, it is not so toxic as plutonium, and it can be used in simple gun-type weapons. These could also appeal to advanced countries as a quick interim measure, especially if testing is not possible.

It would be almost impossible, however, to say unambiguously that a particular investment decision in a civilian nuclear program is tantamount to a decision to produce nuclear weapons. After all, it is not uncommon for countries to install uneconomic industrial facilities for various reasons, including gaining experience with a new technology and national prestige. The insistence on a highly self-sufficient civilian nuclear program does not in itself prove any intentions concerning nuclear weapons.

It is interesting that the present drive for commerical uranium enrichment facilities abroad stems from earlier U.S. success in urging adoption of the more economic U.S.-type enriched uranium reactors, particularly in the Federal Republic of Germany and Japan. Natural uranium is widely available, but so long as the United States has an effective monopoly on commercial enrichment services, diversion of plutonium produced in U.S.-supplied fuel is a rather implausible course. However, the success of the U.S.-type reactors considerably enhanced prospects for the growth of civilian nuclear power and provided industrial countries with strong motives for developing domestic uranium enrichment technology. As we have seen, successful development may now lead to the commercial sale of this technology to a wider class of secondary countries. This would, in effect, give many countries access to highly enriched uranium, which they could employ for military purposes.

Finally, those concerned with nuclear proliferation often want to know the cost of nuclear warheads, usually to assess the prospects for a country to produce them. There is no succinct answer because there is no unique cost of a nuclear warhead, any more than there is of an airplane. However, for those eager to have a number, it is probably reasonably accurate to say $1 million per warhead—or more than several hundred thousand dollars and probably less than several million—with a minimum total program cost for a stockpile of perhaps tens of millions of dollars or more. In any event, the warhead cost will probably be less than the cost of a nuclear weapon delivery system.

5

Technical Capabilities of Safeguards

Herbert Scoville, Jr.

Non-Proliferation Treaty Safeguards

The basic objectives of safeguards as set forth in Article III of the Non-Proliferation Treaty is to prevent the diversion by a non-nuclear weapons state of fissionable material from peaceful uses to nuclear weapons or other nuclear explosive devices. In order to achieve this objective the safeguards would be applied to all source or fissionable material within the state or under its control anywhere. The International Atomic Energy Agency (IAEA) is the organization charged with the responsibility for ensuring that such diversion does not take place.

The IAEA would carry out its safeguarding functions on a national or occasionally on a multinational or regional scale. Where several nations are intimately involved in a nuclear program, there would be greater risks in carrying out a clandestine diversion program. But particularly where allies are involved, the safeguarding organization cannot afford to rely on one nation detecting and revealing diversions by another.

The IAEA would not be responsible for controlling the actions of individuals or organizations within a nation. Thus, for example, each country would be responsible for the physical security necessary to prevent the hijacking of material while in transit from one plant to another or for preventing embezzlement of material by individuals within a plant. If material were missing within a nation, then that nation would be responsible for its loss. The IAEA cannot assume police or custodial powers.

While under Article III safeguards will be applied on all source or fissionable material, a wide variation in the stringency of the safeguarding procedures can exist for different types of materials. The basic purpose of the safeguards is to prevent the manufacture of nuclear explosives so that fissionable materials, plutonium and highly enriched uranium, which can be used directly for these, must be the most carefully monitored. Low enrichment uranium or natural uranium, requiring extensive further processing in reactors or separation plants, do not need the same high degree of accountability or security. Some controls on source materials are extremely useful, since they provide the means of maintaining a material balance throughout the entire nuclear fuel cycle. However, in evaluating the technical capabilities of safeguards, the probability that plutonium or highly enriched uranium can be diverted is of primary concern.

If one looks at it from the point of view of a potential violator of the Non-Proliferation Treaty, this priority is even more apparent. The political and perhaps practical consequences of being detected in a violation would be great, otherwise the nation would merely abrogate the treaty. Even within a nation many people would be opposed to a clandestine program. Therefore, any violation should involve a minimum number of knowledgeable persons, which in turn means a minimum-size clandestine program. The diversion of weapons-grade material, preferably in processed form, best satisfies this criterion, while a diversion program that also requires a clandestine reactor or uranium enrichment plant would run a high risk of being discovered.

While the IAEA would be responsible for applying safeguards to all *declared* materials wherever they might be, it was not the intent for it to be responsible for detecting the existence of or locating any undeclared materials. Clearly the IAEA could not become an international espionage organization or have the right to roam over a country trying to locate clandestine nuclear plants. This does not necessarily mean that there is a serious loophole in the safeguards under the treaty or that the clandestine production of fissionable material would be easy. Any non-nuclear nation that failed to declare a significant amount of source or fissionable material would do so at considerable risk of being caught in a flagrant violation of the treaty. Nuclear plants that manufacture or process fissionable material are quite large, have stringent safety requirements, produce radioactive materials that are easy to detect, and employ appreciable numbers of skilled personnel. All these factors make such plants difficult to conceal. Operation of a clandestine nuclear plant would involve a high risk of being detected by the intelligence services of other nations. For this reason any diversion of fissionable material from safeguarded plants is likely to occur when the material is in a separated form so it can be easily converted into weapons.

Safeguarding Techniques

A wide variety of techniques exists to provide information on whether fissionable material is being diverted from a legitimate peaceful program. Some methods will be useful for certain stages in the fuel cycle and completely unpractical in others. In some cases several methods may be applicable and when used together will compound the difficulty of successfully carrying out a secret diversion to weapons.

However, care must be exercised in applying safeguards to avoid interference with peaceful programs and the disclosure of trade secrets. Such fears created tremendous difficulties in negotiating the safeguards article in the Non-Proliferation Treaty and still give rise to objections to adherence to the treaty. Therefore, the application of any specific technique must be clearly justifiable as providing significant assurance against diversion and not merely information which might be nice to know. Fortunately, with care safeguards can be applied without revealing industrial secrets.

The most generally useful approach is the audit of accounting procedures already being used on a national or industrial basis. Checking records to insure that they are free of mistakes and are consistent at all points is a basic starting point for preventing diversion of fissionable material.

The maintenance of a material balance by measurements insofar as possible at all stages of the fuel cycle is also highly desirable. However, at some stages sufficiently accurate measurements may not be practical, and reliance may have to be placed on other means. Even in the best operated plants, there may be losses or "material unaccounted for" (MUF). For any process, however, experience will provide the normally expected variability in the MUF for a given plant. Furthermore, in almost all cases there will be similar plants in nuclear weapon nations to provide data on reasonable standards for the MUF and its variability for comparison with those obtained in the safeguarded plants of the non-nuclear weapon nations. Any sudden increase in the MUF in such a plant would raise suspicion of diversion and at a minimum provide a basis for more rigorous inspection to determine the cause of the loss.

Agreed criteria to determine when an alarm should be sounded will have to be developed. A major problem could develop if sloppy operating procedures were to exist on a continuing basis in a plant or nuclear program of a country. Such procedures would also be bad from an economic and a safety point of view, but they nevertheless could exist. In such circumstances, it might be necessary for the IAEA to insist on improvements in plant operation or perhaps institute special accounting of its own.

Fundamental to the obtaining of a material balance will be analytical procedures to determine the quantities of fissionable material at various points in the nuclear fuel cycle. Highly sensitive and accurate techniques exist for measuring the isotopic content of materials once they have been placed in solution. The major problem is the selection of statistically meaningful and representative samples of nuclear materials to be analyzed.

For solid materials, such as fuel elements, the problem is more difficult. Typical elements can be randomly selected and dissolved for analysis, but this necessitates destruction of the element. However, extensive research has been under way for some time in the United States and elsewhere on non-destructive assay methods, and there is every reason to believe that satisfactory practical procedures will be available in time for use in safeguarding unirradiated fuels under the Non-Proliferation Treaty. For irradiated fuels a satisfactory method cannot be so clearly anticipated, but fortunately the need is not so critical since the penalties from destructive analysis are less great.

An important tool in safeguards is the numbering and labeling of items or batches of material to prevent removal or substitution and reduce the necessity for frequent isotopic analyses. For example, if a fuel rod can be tagged when manufactured and assayed, then the material in it can be accounted for by mere observation of the identifier as it is stored, shipped, placed in the reactor and, hopefully, even after exposure while it is cooling or being shipped to the chemical reprocessing plant. This latter presents certain technical problems due to the effects of exposure in the reactor, but these are probably solvable at least in many situations.

Minor isotope safeguard techniques (MIST's) are being tested and show considerable promise for certain parts of the fuel cycle. These employ mass spectographic analysis of the less common isotopes of plutonium and uranium which may be present along with the common Pu-239 and U-238. Recent experiments have shown the applicability of these to monitoring materials being processed through chemical reprocessing plants. The techniques could have great value in safeguarding a uranium enrichment plant when such plants come under the safeguards, but they have not yet been tested. In each of these cases the diversion of fissionable materials from the normal process stream would result in a change in the isotopic ratios, which would provide a warning that the diversion was taking place. Attempts to fool the analysis by substitution of minor isotopes would be almost impossible.

Finally, the procedure that is most attractive where practical is containment with tamper-resistant or tamper-indicating seals to provide warning of any attempt to remove the material. This technique involves a minimum of interference with or intrusion into the operation of a nuclear plant. Unlike analytical and accounting procedures, which involve a percentage reliability containment is an all-or-nothing method. Either it works and no material can be diverted or it fails and all the material in the contained volume can be stolen until measurement of the material in the volume can be made. This makes the method particularly useful in the longer range future, when large quantities of material will be handled and diversion of even a small percentage could be significant.

At the present time there is a wide variety of seals that can be used under different circumstances. It is not necessary that these be pick-proof, but only that the seals give evidence that penetration has taken place. It is often more difficult, however, to engineer practically the containment areas to insure that diversion is not occurring. With a batch-fueled reactor, containment is easy, but in a continuous flow processing plant containment is not so readily feasible. In such a situation tamper-resistant instrumentation, such as TV monitors, might be used to detect any clandestine operation. Such systems are already being field tested.

Safeguarding Various Stages in the Fuel Cycle

The risks of diversion and the problems of safeguarding will vary for each stage in the fuel cycle. Likewise, the efficiency and practicality of the various safeguarding techniques will be different for each case. Therefore, it is important to analyze each stage separately. (A diagram of a representative fuel cycle is given in Figure 3 in Victor Gilinsky's "Military Potential of Civilian Nuclear Power" in this volume, and can be used for analysis.)

Mining, Milling, and Conversion

In these stages large quantities of materials are handled, but these have little direct usefulness in producing nuclear weapons without extensive further processing. The risks from diversion are almost non-existent. Therefore, safeguards procedures can be extremely simple and should be designed primarily to obtain a rough value of the input of source material to the remainder of the fuel cycle. In most cases a review of the inventory records would be adequate. In many nations lacking indigenous sources of raw materials this input can be obtained from shipping manifests.

Uranium Enrichment

At the present time all known uranium enrichment plants are located in nuclear weapon countries, so the problem of diversion under the Non-Proliferation Treaty will not be a problem for a number of years. However, the United Kingdom, West Germany, and the Netherlands have recently initiated a project to construct a gas centrifuge plant in the Netherlands to produce enriched uranium for nuclear power programs. Some other countries may follow suit, but the number of such plants will probably always be limited to a few large ones, since otherwise it will be difficult to make them economically justifiable and competitive with existing plants in nuclear weapon countries where much of the original capital investment has been written off already for weapons.

Safeguarding procedures for enrichment plants are still in the study and research phases, since to date there has been no requirement for them. If the plant were designed and operated to produce high enrichment uranium-235, then clearly the safeguards for this part of the fuel cycle must have a high probability of detecting even a small diversion. If the enrichment were limited to a few percent, which would be normal for most nuclear power requirements, safeguards could be somewhat less stringent. But even in this situation the risk of diversion would be significant, since low enrichment material can be raised to weapon-quality material in facilities that might be relatively easy to conceal. While methods are still unproven, it does appear that safeguarding will be technically quite feasible. Containment procedures with careful accounting of the input and output of the plant using existing analytical techniques to determine the isotopic ratios of the materials should be able to keep the risks of diversion to acceptable levels.

Fuel Fabrication

The manufacture of fuel for reactors frequently utilizes enriched uranium (normally a few percent but in some cases highly enriched material) and plutonium in a wide variety of processing and fabrication operations. Furthermore, it is at this stage that considerable scrap can be produced and stored for appreciable periods. All of these factors complicate the safeguarding process, and the employment of a wide variety of techniques will be required. The use of non-destructive assay methods is particularly important to assist in auditing the records and maintaining a material balance. This may also require the use of inspections without advance notice. A fuel element numbering and identification system will be very useful in maintaining accountability at this and later stages. In some types of operations containment will be desirable. It may even be necessary to establish limits on the acceptable amounts of unprocessed scrap in order to keep the material unaccounted for sufficiently low. High MUF and particularly wide variations in MUF during the fuel fabrication cannot be tolerated. While this stage may be as difficult as any to safeguard, it is gratifying to note that a recent panel of the Atomic Industrial Forum that studied safeguarding procedures for this stage was "certain that practices which satisfy the countervailing interests of competent fabricators and knowledgeable customers would prove to be more than adequate for safeguarding purposes."[1]

Reactors

Once fissionable material is in a reactor, the opportunities for diversion are greatly decreased. For batch-loaded reactors, safeguarding is particularly easy. Simple tamper-proof seals on the reactor would eliminate whatever small risk existed. Even these may not be necessary. For continuous refueling reactors safeguarding is less easy, but even so, maintaining accountability on the fuel elements should not prove too difficult. Fuel assemblies are normally large and inventories can be audited without much difficulty. If an indestructible identification and numbering system were used at the time of fabrication of the assembly, this would further simplify the auditing process. Tamper-indicating instrumentation has also been recently tested very successfully in safeguarding such a reactor in Canada. Furthermore, once the fuel elements have been exposed in the reactor they will be highly radioactive and their clandestine removal cannot be easily effected. Occasional spot inspections could still further reduce this risk if it were deemed serious.

Chemical Reprocessing Plants

Provided reasonable care has been exercised in accounting for the fuel assemblies, there should be little opportunity for secret diversion between their fabrication and placement in the dissolver tank of the reprocessing plant. A ready opportunity will exist for accurate analysis of the fissionable materials present once the fuel is dissolved. The input measurements in the dissolver tank can be checked with the separated plutonium, uranium, and other materials in the output of the reprocessing plant. A comparison of the uranium-235 at this point with that in the original fuel will give a value of the uranium-235 burned up in the reactor from which in turn the plutonium produced can be calculated. This can be compared with the plutonium present to check on whether diversion has occurred. In reprocessing, the MUF must also be kept as low as possible, and reasonable norms for variations in MUF must be established. Once the fuel has been processed so as to separate the uranium and plutonium from the radioactive fission products, then the opportunities for diversion will increase. Great care must, therefore, be exercised in establishing good accounting procedures and auditing carefully the input and output of materials. Sloppy procedures could seriously degrade the effectiveness of safeguards, but with good operations the accountability should be maintained to less than 1 per cent. MIST also offers promise here in reducing the risks of diversion. These techniques in combination with containment of much of the plant and surprise inspections, or, if necessary, resident inspectors, provide the capability for keeping the risks of diversion to acceptable levels.

Transportation and Storage

The use of tamper-indicating sealed containers or storage spaces together with serialized indestructible identification techniques can make it virtually impossible for fissionable materials to be diverted without detection during transportation and storage. However, there will always be risks that material will be stolen by individuals or Mafia-type organizations. After theft, the material could be sold internationally on the black market in much the same manner as drugs. The risks of theft are probably highest in nuclear weapon nations where the supplies and shipments of weapons-grade materials are the largest.

It will be the responsibility of the national government, not the IAEA, to implement security procedures to minimize this risk and recover the material if it is missing. Obviously, were this to occur frequently, the safeguards system would break down and worries would develop that the government was conniving in this theft as a means of circumventing the treaty. Other nations would have to examine carefully the circumstances surrounding such a loss to determine whether they viewed it as a violation. To reduce the risks of theft, international standards for shipping procedures should probably be developed. Internal security forces should be alerted to forestall hijacking and to apprehend the culprits if it occurs.

Overall Effectiveness of Safeguards

A review of the entire fuel cycle indicates that only in the fuel fabrication and fuel reprocessing stages are there serious questions about the technical capabilities of safeguards. Even in these two areas, inventory control has the potential of detecting a diversion of a few tenths of a percent, or less, of the throughput of fissionable materials. When such audits are combined with other safeguarding procedures, such as containment, it should be possible to provide a high probability that a diversion of even smaller amounts of material would be discovered. A plant with a throughput of 1,000 kilograms of plutonium per year would probably have to operate five years to allow diversion of enough material for even one bomb. Thus any nation contemplating such a clandestine program would have to be prepared to face up to the consequences of being apprehended in a violation of the Non-Proliferation Treaty.

Fortunately, at least for many years, it is also unlikely that many large plants for reprocessing or fuel fabrication will exist in non-nuclear weapon countries. At the present time, there are only two known reprocessing plants in non-nuclear weapon countries, the internationally owned Eurochemic plant in Belgium and the smaller plant at Trombay, India. Others will undoubtedly be built, for example in Japan, but the number is likely to remain small for economic reasons.

Furthermore, in most nations with large nuclear power programs and the economic base to build large fuel-handling facilities, the diversion of material for a single or a few bombs provides little, if any, military advantage. On the other hand, nuclear power programs in those nations that might desire only a few weapons are likely to be small for many years, so that the opportunities for diversion will also be small. For example, a clandestine program to build a few weapons in such large industrial nations as West Germany or Japan would have little military or political value, and only make them a potential target for nuclear attack. On the other hand, the diversion of enough material for even a few weapons in such nations as Israel and the United Arab Republic would be virtually impossible if their relatively small nuclear programs were properly safeguarded.

In conclusion, it should be emphasized that this rather optimistic forecast of the capabilities for safeguarding peaceful nuclear programs under the Non-Proliferation Treaty is contingent on a number of factors. First, it will be necessary to continue vigorous development of new safeguarding techniques and practices so that they can become realistically operational as the potential for diversion increases. Second, and most important, it assumes that the larger nuclear plants will be operated on an efficient basis so as to keep the material unaccounted for to reasonably low and constant levels. Such operation can be readily justified on an economic basis, and, therefore, will not impose any hardship on the operator. Third, if the risks of diversion are to be kept within bounds, it will be important for the IAEA to support the individual inspectors when they obtain evidence of excessive losses of material and in turn for the member nations to support the IAEA when potential violations are reported. If sloppy operations with consequent excessive losses of material are tolerated, or if evidence of possible violations is allowed to become lost in the international bureaucracy or down-graded by political timidity, then the entire safeguards system will rapidly become a hollow shell.

The potential technical capabilities of safeguards are adequate to reduce to acceptable levels the risk of significant diversion of fissionable materials to weapons at least for many years to come. However, these capabilities will be realized only by a determined common effort on the part of many nations.

6   EURATOM and the IAEA

Lawrence Scheinman

The principle of international safeguards applied to peaceful nuclear activities has gained increasing legitimacy over the years, but its implementation has been divided between regional and more universal efforts. The Non-Proliferation Treaty posed the difficult problem of reconciling two existing international safeguards systems: one developed by the International Atomic Energy Agency (IAEA), a quasi-universal international organization and member of the United Nations family; and one administered through the more limited European Atomic Energy Community (EURATOM), of which only France, West Germany, Italy, Belgium, the Netherlands, and Luxembourg are members.

While the EURATOM states were sympathetic to the principle of non-proliferation and most of them prepared to accept the obligations flowing from adherence to a non-proliferation agreement, they were unwilling to yield their regional safeguards system to the broader IAEA system for reasons examined below. During the Non-Proliferation Treaty negotiations, this issue involved primarily the United States, the Soviet Union, and the EURATOM states, with the United States seeking to satisfy both Moscow and its West European allies. With the coming into force of the treaty on March 5, 1970, and the commencement of the two-year period during which the parties are to negotiate safeguards agreements with the IAEA, we move from general principles to implementation and the number of interested nations increases

The author would like to extend his sincere thanks to the Carnegie Endowment for International Peace for its generosity in providing its facilities and the time in which to prepare this study.

significantly. The purpose in the following pages is to try to analyze some of the dimensions of the problem of accommodating these two competitive safeguards systems and of implementing the provisions contained in Article III of the treaty which sets forth the safeguards requirements.

Evolution

Safeguards were incorporated in the Non-Proliferation Treaty at the insistence of the United States in keeping with a long-standing policy of controlled nuclear development. Earlier drafts of Article III were permissive in nature: the United States called for "the application of International Atomic Energy Agency or equivalent international safeguards," implicitly preserving the EURATOM system (draft of August 17, 1965), and the Soviet Union went only so far as to call for a commitment by signatory states not to encourage or assist nuclear proliferation (draft of September 24, 1966). By 1967, however, the Soviet Union had come to insist that safeguards be obligatory and universal and to argue that only the IAEA system could meet this requirement. The United States, giving precedence to universal over regional goals, drafted a safeguards article that essentially subordinated any other inspection system to IAEA control.

EURATOM's reaction, solicited by the United States under the U.S.-EURATOM Agreement for Cooperation of 1959, was negative, on the ground that the draft article introduced discrimination into the European community and threatened the integrity of the movement toward European integration. A subsequent U.S. draft reintroduced the concept of regional inspection, but subjected it to a proviso that if no agreement were reached between EURATOM and the IAEA within three years of the treaty's coming into force, the IAEA system would automatically apply on the territory of the European Communities. By October, 1967, the EURATOM countries managed to compose their internal differences and to present a community position on the safeguards problem in the form of five conditions that would have to be met if the EURATOM states were to consider the Non-Proliferation Treaty compatible with the EURATOM Treaty. Some of these conditions (such as elimination of the above so-called guillotine clause) were met in the treaty provision ultimately agreed to by the United States and the Soviet Union. Other conditions (e.g., assurance of continued fuel supply from the United States during the period of negotiating a safeguards agreement) were accommodated through private understandings with the United States. The final text of Article III, however, is ambiguous in form, reflecting not only the inability of the superpowers fully to agree on the respective roles of IAEA and EURATOM in the implementation of the Non-Proliferation Treaty, but also their desire not to allow potential differences of interpretation to impede further the submission of a complete draft treaty to the ENDC.

Article III of the Non-Proliferation Treaty provides in part that all non-nuclear weapon parties undertake to "accept safeguards, as set forth in an agreement to be negotiated with the International Atomic Energy Agency," and that such agreements be concluded either individually or collectively. The provision for negotiation implies a certain flexibility in the concluding of safeguarding arrangements, and the reference to the possibility of groups of states entering into such negotiations with the IAEA allows EURATOM to deal as a single entity with the IAEA.

The difficulty in implementing Article III lies less in the principles set forth above than in the further provision that safeguards shall be for the "exclusive purpose of verification of the fulfillment . . . of obligations assumed under this Treaty." Here the issue becomes one of interpretation and application of the concept of *verification*–the concept that facilitated eventual agreement on the control provision in the treaty. Does verification encompass merely a review of the records maintained by an organization such as EURATOM with respect to the receipt, production, and use of source or special fissionable material, and thus imply verification of the EURATOM safeguarding *system* as such? Or does it extend to the right of *independent* access to the territory and facilities of states under these safeguards, thus providing for *autonomous* verification of the effectiveness of the intervening system? The underlying issue of course is political, rather than technical, effectiveness. What is politically effective is, in the last analysis, a question of confidence, credibility, and parity.

Thus far there have been few preliminary public interpretations of the meaning of Article III insofar as it deals with *interorganizational* relationships. The United States did enunciate guiding principles regarding Article III in January, 1968, indicating that in its view the safeguards agreements negotiated should be such that all parties can have confidence in their effectiveness, and that "the IAEA should make appropriate use of existing records and safeguards" to avoid unnecessary duplication, provided that the IAEA can satisfy itself that diversion is not taking place. The term "appropriate use" is as vulnerable and ambiguous as the concept of "verification," and there is a real question whether "appropriate use" of an intervening safeguards system can in fact satisfy the political requirement that all parties have confidence in the implementation of the treaty obligations.

EURATOM unofficially has interpreted these guiding principles liberally as meeting their demand that the arrangement negotiated should concern the verification of EURATOM safeguarding methods and not entail direct IAEA control. Similarly, the government of the Federal Republic of Germany, upon its signing of the treaty in November, 1969, did so on the understanding "that the agreements between IAEA and EURATOM, as described in Article III of the Non-Proliferation Treaty, shall be concluded on the basis of the principle of verification, and that verification shall take place in a way that does not affect the tasks [of EURATOM] in the political, scientific, economic and technical fields."

The Soviet Union has not tabled interpretive statements regarding Article III in anything more than a general way, although a Soviet official has stated that the provisions of the statute of IAEA would be applied to agreements concluded under Article III and that the statute gives IAEA "considerable authority to observe how the safeguards agreements are complied with by States which have concluded such agreements with it." What is undoubtedly more disconcerting to the EURATOM states, however, is the Soviet Union's long-standing antipathy to EURATOM and to European integration in general. Thus, Moscow has characterized EURATOM as nothing more than a "closed organization of West Germany's allies in the military NATO bloc," and for a long time it refused to vote in favor of granting EURATOM observer status at the annual conferences of the IAEA on the ground that it was not devoted to purely peaceful purposes. Although the Soviet Union remained silent on EURATOM at the 1969 IAEA General Conference, the Bulgarian delegation, presumably speaking for other Communist bloc states as well, declared itself against "acceptance of the principle of regional safeguards systems, which in practice would lead to countries applying safeguards to themselves." EURATOM obviously will not be able to look to Eastern Europe for support of its claims.

Two Levels of Action

Analysis of IAEA-EURATOM safeguarding relationships must consider two levels of action involving theoretically autonomous, but de facto interdependent, actors. First, there is the question of the negotiations that must take place within EURATOM between its member states with a view to establishing a common position on a mandate for negotiating a safeguards agreement with the IAEA. Second, there is the matter of negotiations between EURATOM and the IAEA, which cannot be reduced to the simple equation of interorganizational trade-offs. In a real sense, the IAEA-EURATOM negotiations are negotiations between a supranational community claiming special treatment for itself and all other nations who are parties to the Non-Proliferation Treaty. These negotiations will be important for the precedents they set not only for interorganization relationships, but for how the IAEA will treat with individual adherents as well. A striking example of this aspect of the problem, as we shall see, is Japan.

Linked to these two problems is the question of how far EURATOM should be allowed to go in invoking its constitutional structure and decision-making process as a defense against deviation from self-imposed instructions on what it can and cannot accept. The processes by which the European communities reach agreement are complex, since the interests of six fundamentally independent nation-states must be accommodated. But there is always a risk that this will become a convenient excuse for doing less than others or for pressing for exceptional treatment.

This may pose a problem particularly for the United States. Throughout the postwar period the United States has given strong support to West European integration. In pursuit of this policy it negotiated special safeguards arrangements whereby EURATOM took over functions that otherwise would have been performed by it. When individual bilateral agreements between the United States and EURATOM countries expired in the mid- and late sixties, Washington transferred safeguarding responsibilities under renewal agreements to EURATOM, thus strengthening the hand of that organization and attesting to the confidence of the United States in the effectiveness of the EURATOM system. It may thus fall to the United States, which is accepting international safeguards voluntarily, to show the way to EURATOM by negotiating a model agreement with the IAEA designed to maximize the effectiveness of a universal safeguards system. While the cases of EURATOM and the United States are not identical, EURATOM's ability to claim special treatment would be weakened to the extent that other parties to the treaty which need not do so accepted a liberal interpretation of IAEA's role and authority. Against this background we can now turn to an examination of the two levels of action.

Intra-EURATOM Problems

Effect on Integration

Prior to any negotiation between EURATOM and the IAEA under Article III of the Non-Proliferation Treaty, agreement must be reached among the EURATOM states with respect to a negotiating mandate for the commission that will act on their behalf. The history of EURATOM amply demonstrates its nonmonolithic character. Despite internal differences of opinion, however, the community has managed to present a fairly solid front throughout the treaty negotiations. This is both surprising and comprehensible.

It is surprising in the sense that almost since its inception and particularly since 1964 EURATOM has been in a state of constant crisis. Its second five-year research program was progressively deflated as member states refused to reinforce its weakening financial and programmatic base, and the community was unable to agree to a third pluriannual program when the second terminated in 1967. Since that time, EURATOM has been carried, on a sharply reduced basis, by transitory annual programs. Despite numerous commitments by the Council of Ministers to reach agreement on some kind of long-term program, the community remained, at least through 1969, in a state of limbo. In the long view, EURATOM's record of cohesion has not been strong and its contribution to European integration in any positive sense of the term has been negligible. Sharply diverging interests, clashing nationalist orientations in both political and economic terms, and weak leadership have all contributed to making EURATOM more distinguished for its failures than for its successes.

What makes the relatively high degree of EURATOM cohesion comprehensible is the fact that the Non-Proliferation Treaty represents an external challenge, not merely to EURATOM but to the entire complex of European community institutions of which it is a part. At least this is how the issue is perceived by many Europeans. The presentation by the United States of the draft Article III referred to earlier in which non-nuclear weapon parties were called upon to "accept the safeguards of the IAEA on all . . . peaceful nuclear activities" stimulated the community to take action in its own defense. The arguments that were raised on behalf of EURATOM are fundamentally the same that have sustained the EURATOM claim for special consideration through the present time: EURATOM had a proven and effective security control system that applied uniformly and in a non-discriminatory fashion to all members of the community, whether nuclear-weapon states or not. Any disruption of the non-discrimination principle by the intervention of a superordinate safeguarding system that exempted states from inspection because of their nuclear-weapon status not only would establish legal barriers in the existing nuclear common market and undermine the principle of equal access to source and fissionable materials on a non-discriminatory basis, but also would undermine the foundations upon which European integration was being built. (We leave out of consideration for the purposes of this discussion the security issue and those aspects of the political dimensions of the problem of European integration that relate to the impact of the Non-Proliferation Treaty per se, and especially Articles I and II, on the eventual development of a European nuclear force, since our major concern here is with Article III and the safeguards issue.)

Observers of the state of European politics in the mid-1960's might well regard some of these contentions with cynicism in view of the *malaise* that characterized the European communities, the reassertion of nationalism in Gaullist France and elsewhere, the stalemate in the movement for political integration and the increasing concern over the viability of what economic integration already had taken place. In the technological sectors in general, and in the nuclear sector in particular, there was little if any evidence of trans-European linkages or mergers, and wasteful competition pervaded the field of reactor development both for proven reactors and for the future breeders.

What most critics then failed to see, and what is still less than fully appreciated even today, Europeans will argue, is that however weak the EURATOM venture has proven thus far it is an integral part of a much broader enterprise. While not the keystone in the arch of European integration, EURATOM is one of the building blocks whose destruction or further weakening could have a serious psychological impact on the outlook of political leadership in Western Europe and, consequently, on the promise for a more closely integrated Western Europe. It is thus at the less tangible and more symbolic aspects that one must look in evaluating the political claims emanating from the European communities.

Even if one is inclined to accept much of this argument in the abstract, daily events in the life of the European communities tend to cast doubt on the future of EURATOM. Faced with the increasingly serious problem of creating independent sources of nuclear fuel in order to compete with American firms in the commercial reactor market, two EURATOM countries—West Germany and the Netherlands—have entered into an agreement with the United Kingdom, still only a candidate for membership in the European communities, to create an independent capability of enriching uranium through the gas centrifuge process instead of accepting an alternative French proposal to enlarge the French diffusion plants at Pierrelatte into EURATOM enriched-uranium facilities. While this tripartite agreement does not preclude the eventual development of a EURATOM plant it does to some extent threaten to undermine the community's plans to create community-wide industrial facilities in the nuclear fields. In circumstances such as these one has reason to question the substance of the claims of the Europeans regarding the importance of EURATOM.

Since the emergence of the non-proliferation issue there have been basically three groupings within EURATOM: (a) West Germany coupled with the commission, (b) France, and (c) the Benelux countries. Italy has vacillated between the first and third groups and does not appear to have as yet determined what its priorities are. The groups themselves have not always been stable, but in the long view this simplified scheme appears to represent the main pattern of alignment.

France

France ranks among the EURATOM states least concerned about the implications of the Non-Proliferation Treaty for peaceful nuclear development, the future of European integration, and national security. In distinguishing between nuclear powers and non-nuclear powers and in defining the former so as to include France, the treaty legitimates France's long-standing claim to great power status and gives to France the recognition she had sought in the nuclear-political field for nearly a decade. If anything, France stands to gain by the treaty, not only in terms of status and prestige, but in functional terms as well. The treaty reinforces France's policy of keeping West Germany in a non-nuclear status and it enhances France's European position insofar as it undermines the kind of nuclear sharing arrangement that the Multi-Lateral Force (MLF) would have brought about. The imposition of a universal control system on all non-nuclear weapon states would discriminate against France's EURATOM partners and in her favor. Whether it also would bring about industrial relocation from German or Italian to French (uninspected) territory in order to avoid the inconveniences, cost, and alleged risk of industrial espionage deriving from safeguarding, as some have argued, seems doubtful. But the adverse effect it might have on the emergence of a nuclear industrial policy for the European communities appears more real.

In light of French disinterest in EURATOM insofar as it served as an entrée for American nuclear technology into the European communities and the general European policies pursued by France under General de Gaulle, it is not surprising that when in 1967 the United States submitted the draft Article III referred to earlier to EURATOM, France contested the right of the community to respond *qua* EURATOM, or even to discuss the non-proliferation issue in the context of the community institutions. While other EURATOM members agreed with France that questions of European security and disarmament or arms control were beyond EURATOM's purview, they did not agree insofar as the question of safeguards on peaceful nuclear activities was concerned. France did not challenge the right of member states to notify the commission of their intention to sign the Non-Proliferation Treaty and to ask whether the latter would contravene their obligations under the EURATOM treaty (a duty of each state under Article 103 of that treaty). But it did contest what Paris considered to be a reversal of procedure—the calling upon the community to serve as a forum for discussing the non-proliferation issue and on the commission to evaluate the latter in light of the EURATOM treaty *prior* to any of the member states taking a position with regard to the Non-Proliferation Treaty. The French did not press the issue however, anticipating that if they withdrew to the sidelines and let the five hash it out between themselves, the lack of community consensus on the treaty would rapidly emerge and reduce the scope of common agreement. The weaker the consensus within EURATOM and the greater the pressure of the United States for acceptance of universal as opposed to regional controls, the higher the probability for vindication of the Gaullist claim that Europe should disengage itself from the Atlantic bloc and assert its own independent policy. If the five succumbed to American pressure then EURATOM would be correspondingly weakened. If they did not, then the opportunity to assert French leadership and direction might be enhanced. Either way France did not stand to lose and the possibility of gains was significant.

To what extent, if at all, has the departure of General de Gaulle affected the French position? It is not clear that a thoroughgoing evaluation of French policy in this field has yet been undertaken at the highest levels of government. This is a difficult question to assess. On the one hand, despite some indications that pressures may be mounting in France in favor of signing the treaty, the Pompidou government continues to maintain an anti-treaty posture. Even if France were to become a party to the treaty, its status as a nuclear weapon state exempts it from the safeguards provisions of Article III, which only a voluntary submission could change. It is here that the French problem becomes increasingly complex. What the Non-Proliferation Treaty gave to France in the sense of legitimating her nuclear status, the EURATOM treaty takes away to the extent that it commits France to accepting equality with its non-nuclear weapon partners in the peaceful nuclear realm, especially with respect to safeguards. France after de Gaulle, if a less dramatic participant in international politics, is not necessarily insensitive to questions of status and prestige. Therefore, it is not to be ruled out of question that the current French government might consider pursuing a policy wherein it becomes a party to the Non-Proliferation Treaty while simultaneously seeking to weaken such controls over French peaceful nuclear facilities as EURATOM now has with the ultimate intention of offering, in the style of such other nuclear powers as the United States and Great Britain, to place some of its facilities under IAEA controls. In this manner, the French goal of reinforcing surveillance over German nuclear development is achieved while France, acting the role of a nuclear power, slips out of the equalizing framework of EURATOM.

On the other hand, two considerations have intervened between de Gaulle's departure and the present time, either or both of which could affect French attitudes toward EURATOM and thus strengthen the case for special consideration that the community will put forward in Vienna. One is the abandonment by France of the gas-graphite reactor series and the decision, taken this past November, to shift to proven-type enriched uranium reactors. The second is the outcome of the Hague summit meeting held in December, 1969, among the heads of state and government of the member states of the European communities. This meeting led to a renewed commitment to reinforce nuclear cooperation among the six and to open possibilities for a genuine European nuclear industry, although the tripartite gas centrifuge agreement discussed earlier raises some questions in this regard. The French reactor decision opens the possibility that France might eventually come to terms with the German consortium of Siemans-AEG and move toward the development of a European-wide nuclear industry in lieu of the compartmentalized bilateral licensing arrangements between European countries and the United States that characterize the current situation. Should the European alternative materialize, the importance of maintaining the integrity of the nuclear common market will be reinforced (assuming that the value of European integration is shared by others), adding credibility to EURATOM's claims.

Whether French thinking has moved this far remains problematical. First, one must give consideration to the "status politics" hypothesis discussed above. Second, one must not exclude the possibility that France might find any IAEA activity on French soil untenable and that, despite the absence of overt hostility to EURATOM, France might consider any potential arrangements between the latter and IAEA unsatisfactory because of access, however minimal, IAEA might acquire to French nuclear industry through its surveillance of EURATOM. From an industrial and commercial point of view France might consider the best course of action to be one that reduces EURATOM controls over its peaceful industry, and thus attempt to undermine efforts now being made to strengthen the community's control system as part of its effort to improve credibility in its bid to gain special status under the non-proliferation regime. In short, one must not underestimate the possibility that industrial considerations may undermine whatever good intentions political leadership may have.

West Germany

The case of West Germany is quite different and even more complex than that of France. If the central purpose of the Non-Proliferation Treaty is to prevent horizontal proliferation, the Bonn government is a central object of that purpose, especially from the point of view of the Soviet Union. For West Germany, the treaty as a whole raises more difficult problems than it does for many others precisely because of Germany's status in the postwar world and the nature of its relationship with the Soviet Union and Eastern Europe. As a divided nation in a divided Europe and the incessant target of Soviet power and propaganda, West Germany logically is concerned about the implications of the treaty for its national security, for its alliance relationships, for the scope and certainty of the commitments of its nuclear allies, and for the *quid* it is entitled to seek from the Soviet bloc on such issues as the non-use of force, the status of Berlin, and the nature of future East-West relationships.

Thus, for Bonn, acceptance of the Non-Proliferation Treaty is not merely the reassertion of an earlier (1954) commitment not to pick up the nuclear option. Rather it is a medium for altering or ameliorating the pattern of East-West politics that has dominated the postwar period by improving relations with the Soviet Union and putting to rest the chronic concern of the Eastern bloc that revanchism or nuclear military aspirations lurk in the wings of the German political stage. All of this is complicated, of course, by the nature of Bonn's links to the United States and to the European communities, as well as by the aspirations and expectations of the Soviet Union in setting forth proposals for a general European security conference.

What EURATOM will accept in the way of a safeguards agreement with the IAEA, therefore, depends in large measure on what West Germany is willing to accept. The protocol associated with the German signature on the Non-Proliferation Treaty, as we noted, contains a series of assumptions and understandings by Bonn among which are declarations regarding the nature of the agreement to be reached (e.g., "agreements . . . shall be concluded on the basis of the principle of verification . . . safeguards shall only be applied to source and special fissionable material and in conformity with the principle of safeguarding effectively the flow of [such] materials at certain strategic points") and a requirement that a satisfactory safeguards agreement must be reached before West Germany will ratify the treaty. Indeed, all five of the non-nuclear EURATOM states accompanied their signature of the treaty with the reservation that ratification by any of them would be conditioned on a satisfactory agreement being reached with the IAEA.

As of now the Bonn government is taking a hard line—harder than some of its EURATOM partners would like. However, when one considers the variety of other goals and objectives the German government entertains, and the possible linkages Bonn might make between safeguards and other agreements, it becomes clear that interesting trade-offs might be in the offing. The discussions in the German Bundestag in November, 1969, and thereafter indicate that another condition precedent to ratification may be the conclusion of a bilateral agreement with the Soviet Union on the renunciation of the use of force, including an explicit disclaimer by the Soviet Union of a right to intervene in Germany under the "enemy states" clauses of the UN Charter (a claim made at the time of the Czech crisis of 1968). Bonn also would want the support of Moscow for its claim to a permanent seat on the Board of Governors of the IAEA—a position that has increasing importance as it is the board that makes determinations regarding safeguards agreements, the safeguards system itself, and any modifications or amendments to either the system or the negotiated agreements.

It is questionable whether Bonn will be able to extract all of these *quids* from the Soviet Union and simultaneously maintain a very restrictive posture on safeguards. It is also possible that efforts by the West German government to link all of these disparate elements together might boomerang. Moscow could endeavor to interpret all of these factors as an effort by Bonn to prevent implementation of the Non-Proliferation Treaty. In any event, it cannot be ruled out that Bonn might agree to a more flexible arrangement with the IAEA than now appears to be the case.

Benelux Countries

The West German position is not fully shared by the Benelux countries, the third of the three groupings noted earlier. The Netherlands in particular has been anxious to ratify the Non-Proliferation Treaty upon which it appears to place a great deal of moral weight. At the time the EURATOM countries were discussing the United States *aide-mémoire* on a draft Article III, the Netherlands argued forcefully that the community must accept a real verification of its control by the IAEA, claiming that while they wished to preserve EURATOM control they felt that a certain subordination of EURATOM to the IAEA was both feasible and perhaps inevitable. They suggested that EURATOM accept a provision to the effect that "each non-nuclear weapon state undertakes to accept IAEA safeguards for the exclusive purpose of verification . . . ." Correspondingly, they rejected a German draft calling upon non-nuclear weapon states to undertake "safeguards *as set forth in agreements* negotiated and concluded with the IAEA."

While Belgium was then less intransigent than the Netherlands, the two came to an accommodation ultimately expressed in a recent Benelux memorandum suggesting a flexible mandate for the commission based upon the principle that the IAEA should exercise no direct control, but be allowed to verify data assembled by the commission through its own inspection procedures (data being defined in such a manner as to exclude any data that could lead to spreading economic or technical knowledge) with some allowance, if good cause is shown, for the IAEA to conduct an on-site inspection. Although this brings Benelux close to the German view, it is important to note that the general attitude of the Netherlands is that, however valuable EURATOM may be, priority ought to be given to arms control and disarmament and that it is better to contribute to this goal than to seek to preserve the status quo.

Conclusion

One new element in the EURATOM equation is the Brandt government. The Kiesinger-Brandt grand coalition took an exceptionally slow and cautious approach to the treaty, raising multiple arguments about technological interference, excessive costs, industrial espionage, or the undermining of European unity as reasons for delaying signature of the treaty. The Brandt government, with its signature of the treaty, its vigorous commitments to amelioration of tension with the East, and its emergence as a progressive element in renewed efforts toward European unification (as demonstrated at the Hague summit meetings of the Six in December, 1969) projects an image of enlightened leadership and an end to the policy of *suivisme* that characterized the Kiesinger government's attitude toward France. The emergence of a German government that takes progressive and "European" action has been well received on the continent and this may enhance Germany's possibilities for exerting strong influence on the outcome of IAEA-EURATOM negotiations. A hard line, in other words, might be accepted somewhat more readily by countries such as the Netherlands than was previously the case because of the compensating factor of the nature and direction of German political leadership.

By way of a brief summary, we can note that the EURATOM states appear agreed not to accept direct controls by the IAEA and not to ratify the Non-Proliferation Treaty until such time as a satisfactory agreement has been reached on safeguards between the two organizations. EURATOM member states are not in full agreement on how far to go in negotiating this agreement, nor on how much latitude should be afforded to the European commission in conducting these negotiations. They are determined to preserve the principle of non-discrimination to the extent possible (insofar as intracommunity relations are concerned and vis-à-vis the outside world as well), but they are somewhat less in agreement on what the impact of the loss of a control function for EURATOM really would be. West Germany and the commission imply immediate, tangible, and direct negative effects while the Benelux countries seem to stop at the psychological impact level. Where, in all this, the line between firm commitment and tactical bargaining positions is to be drawn remains to be seen.

EURATOM-IAEA Relations

If EURATOM and the IAEA were the only two parties involved in the negotiation of a safeguard arrangement it is not improbable that a mutually satisfactory solution would be found without great difficulty. Nevertheless, it is interesting to note that the director-general of the IAEA has on several occasions argued against the principle of regional safeguards on the ground that they have spatially limited credibility and undermine efforts for establishing universal controls. The negotiations in question, however, will not take place in a vacuum. At the very least the EURATOM-IAEA agreement will serve as a model for arrangements between the agency and other regional organizations or groups of states. It is also becoming increasingly clear that individual states negotiating agreements with the IAEA are more than likely to demand equal treatment with EURATOM. Japan already has done so. Thus, the EURATOM-IAEA negotiations will be precedent-setting. It follows from this that however sympathetic to EURATOM one may be, and however much confidence one may have in the effectiveness of its control system, the interests of the Non-Proliferation Treaty may best be served by an agreement that maximizes the capabilities of the international safeguards system.

How far the IAEA can go in accommodating EURATOM depends on several factors. First, there is the question of what one expects from a safeguards system. If the purpose is to keep nations honest by constantly reminding them that they are under frequent surveillance so as to deter moral corruption on their part, it might be possible to depend upon a fairly flexible system in which the IAEA will count heavily upon what others do in the way of inspection. If, on the other hand, the purpose is to maximize the effectiveness of a single international inspectorate then it may be necessary to vest that inspectorate with wide-ranging independent powers, thus reducing reliance upon intervening inspection systems. This latter alternative assumes that moral deterrence is weak and that one must go beyond providing a system in which nations have the opportunity to demonstrate their good faith and their respect of the treaty obligations. It is the difference between a deterrent-oriented and a detection-oriented system that is at issue here.

Second, there is the question of what it will take to provide the necessary credibility for an international safeguards system. Quite obviously what is acceptable to one state vis-à-vis another may not be acceptable to a third. The United States may (and does) consider the EURATOM system to be an effective and acceptable control over the problem of diversion. The Soviet Union may not (and from the past record does not) take the same view. A regional system that incorporated both India and Pakistan might be acceptable to both and to outsiders, but one that included only India (assuming India were to participate eventually in the system) to the exclusion of Pakistan well might not satisfy the latter. Insofar as EURATOM is concerned there is a real question whether the Soviet bloc ultimately will accept what EURATOM will demand. The West European-East European relationship is an adversary one, not the relatively harmonious kind that characterizes European-American relations. It certainly is not to be expected that the Soviets either perceive things in the same way or would be willing to accept precisely the same kinds of commitments as would the United States.

The Soviet position toward EURATOM-IAEA negotiations promises to be important. Even if one take the optimistic view that the Soviet interest in detente with the United States and the West is real (whether as a result of her problems with China, or out of a desire to consolidate the status quo in Eastern Europe), there is no basis for assuming that the Soviet Union will pass up opportunities to weaken cohesion within the Western camp, (whether in the West European or the Atlantic contexts). This would be a matter of good politics rather than of bad faith. The EURATOM-IAEA negotiations provide one opportunity to the Soviet Union to pursue her long-standing objective of putting obstacles in the path of West European integration and of loosening the links between the latter and the United States.

One example of potential difficulty is the concept of "strategic points," which was introduced into the preamble of the Non-Proliferation Treaty at the urging of the Bonn government. There have thus far been no authentic interpretations of the strategic points concept, but it undoubtedly will evoke different interpretations. By definition, strategic points is a limiting, exclusionary concept designed to make inspection and safeguards less rather than more intrusive. Clearly it will be in the interest of those parties to the treaty who are most supportive of the concept to define it to mean that inspection shall take place only at such points in the fuel cycle as are designated as "strategic." Whether the Soviet Union, for example, would accept a definition that permanently excluded international inspectors from access to areas between these points, or whether they would even accept an interpretation that minimized the number of points in a fuel cycle to be designated as "strategic" is an open question. In any event it is not hard to imagine the difficulties that could arise in putting the concept into operation.

Another difficulty, somewhat more remote but nevertheless possible, may arise from the German understanding that "until the conclusion of the agreement between the IAEA and EURATOM, the supply contracts concluded between EURATOM and the Parties to the Non-Proliferation Treaty shall remain in force. . . ." Here, the question that arises is what happens if the time for negotiation of agreements specified in the treaty has expired without a satisfactory agreement having been reached?* Presumably, Germany, and hence perhaps EURATOM, will interpret this understanding to *not* be limited by this fact, but would the Soviet Union be inclined to agree? Probably not. What is more, the position of the United States is also in doubt,

---

*Although from a legal point of view the time for negotiating a safeguards agreement does not begin to run until ratification, the EURATOM states, having created their own conditions for ratification, are politically ill-placed to press the legal argument and are bound to make every effort to reach accommodation with the IAEA by March, 1972. It also should be remembered that the EURATOM countries' commitment to each other not to ratify the Non-Proliferation Treaty prior to reaching an acceptable agreement with IAEA is not immutable in the sense that some of the EURATOM states are more anxious than others to implement that Treaty and thus place a higher value on non-proliferation than on the particular nuclear aspects of regional integration. The tenuous nature of EURATOM cohesion on this issue undoubtedly will serve as a constraint on the Community to facilitate rather than impede negotiations with IAEA.

despite the fact that the German understanding is based on consultations with Washington. In his testimony before the Senate Foreign Relations Committee in July, 1968, Secretary of State Rusk stated with regard to U.S. supply obligations that "In the event that a non-nuclear-weapon country, whether signatory or not, does not conclude a safeguards agreement with the IAEA, we would of course feel obliged to review the situation in light of the existing circumstances." How the United States would interpret this statement in the conditions of 1972, for example, is clearly difficult to say.

Our point here is only to suggest that many of the ambiguities in the treaty and in interpretative statements hold promise for those who would seek to create tensions between various signatory states. And, as stated before, even a well-intentioned Soviet Union would be obliged to take advantage of these opportunities if to do so would serve any of the long-range diplomatic goals. As the maximization of Soviet influence and the minimization of American influence in Europe is one of those goals, one would anticipate the Soviet Union seizing such opportunities as were presented.

There is a third range of problems flowing from the EURATOM case that not only might serve to minimize the need for Soviet harassment in the safeguards field, but also may prove to be the principal problem the community will have to face in negotiating a safeguards agreement with the IAEA. This is the problem of general non-discrimination and parity treatment. Here, the principal protagonist is Japan which, upon signing the Non-Proliferation Treaty on February 3, 1970, stated that:

> The safeguards agreement to be concluded by Japan with the International Atomic Energy Agency in accordance with Article III of the treaty must not be such as would subject her to disadvantageous treatment as compared with the safeguards agreements which other states' parties conclude with the same Agency, *either individually or together with other states.* (Emphasis added.)

Thus Japan has put the treaty signatories on notice that it expects to be treated in the same way as EURATOM. The *Washington Post* reported on December 15, 1969, that at a meeting of technical specialists on safeguards in Tokyo in December, the Japanese concluded that EURATOM inspection amounts to "friends inspecting each other," and argued that, if this is acceptable for West Germany, then it also should be acceptable for Japan. This is not so much a question of political differences or of credibility as a concern for parity in peaceful nuclear development and industrial and commercial competition.

In one sense, the Japanese demands unnecessarily complicate EURATOM's task. If the European communities had in fact developed a very high degree of *political* integration, along the lines of a confederal arrangement or beyond, then the Japanese argument would have some credibility. But by any objective standard this is not the case and the probabilities of a United States of Europe remain the vision of a very distant future. Until such time as that vision begins to take on a clear and distinct shape contentions that EURATOM inspection is a matter of "friends inspecting each other" will have very little foundation in fact. Furthermore, in EURATOM it is not a case of a German inspector inspecting Karlsruhe or some other German nuclear facility—it is a matter of Frenchmen inspecting Germans.

The problem, however, is that objective analysis is not likely to take precedence in the case of safeguards arrangements. This is a political matter, deeply impregnated with economic and technological implications. Commercial competition, world markets, and economically beneficial technological advancements are some of the issues at stake. So is the political pride of the states that must submit to safeguards arrangements.

The offers of the United States and the United Kingdom to place themselves on a par with the non-nuclear weapon states insofar as inspection is concerned alleviate to a degree these problems. But in doing so they may raise more difficulties than they resolve. Here one enters into the realm of costs, of the rationality of applying the same standards to a nuclear weapon state as to a non-nuclear weapon state, and of the ultimate level at which one may therefore have to set safeguards in order to keep them within manageable bounds. For the purposes of this discussion the important point is that EURATOM faces not only the suspicion of the East Europeans, but the demands for equal treatment by other technologically advanced states.

Part of the difficulty may be resolved by the intensive development of an even more effective EURATOM system complete with automation, resident inspection (in the case of fabrication and processing plants as well as of enrichment installations) and generally highly sophisticated materials management systems. Whether even this, however, will satisfy the great majority of Non-Proliferation Treaty signatories remains problematical, for we are dealing with an area heavily laden with the problems of symbolic politics.

7 Assurance of International Safeguards

John Gorham Palfrey

Nature of the Assurance

It may sometimes sound rather improbable, on the face of the proposal, for just three of the five nuclear weapon countries to call upon all the non-nuclear weapon countries of the world to sign a treaty to agree not to develop the nuclear weapons which all five nuclear weapon powers have already developed and are continuing to develop. It may sound still more improbable to call upon the non-nuclear weapon powers, in addition, to accept mandatory international safeguards on their own lawful, peaceful nuclear activities to assure the nuclear weapon countries, and each other, that they will not secretly divert the fissionable material, that they are using and producing for civilian purposes, to build bombs—especially when the nuclear weapon countries are accepting no such inspection as part of the bargain. Nevertheless, these are the terms of the Non-Proliferation Treaty.

While observations about the asymmetry of the treaty are often over-stated—because there are genuine commitments by the nuclear weapon powers and gains for all—complaints are not surprising. What, after all, do the nuclear powers really give up? What do the non-nuclear powers acquire, except a commitment to a series of self-denying ordinances, and a required international inspection system that could lead to inconvenience, expense, and possible loss of trade secrets in a competitive nuclear power world market?

Thus one quickly arrives at the question of the perils created and the assurances provided with regard to peaceful nuclear activities of the non-nuclear weapon powers under the Non-Proliferation Treaty, which requires mandatory international inspection.

The central aim of the safeguards provisions in Article III of the treaty is assurance against diversion of fissionable material involved in a non-nuclear weapon country's lawful, peaceful nuclear activities to build bombs, or "peaceful" nuclear explosives, which are essentially indistinguishable from bombs. Under Article III each non-nuclear weapon state undertakes to accept international safeguards on all source and fissionable material within its territory pursuant to agreements to be negotiated with the International Atomic Energy Agency (IAEA). Both nuclear and non-nuclear weapon parties undertake not to export nuclear material or equipment to any non-nuclear weapon state for peaceful purposes, unless the material is subject to international safeguards. Non-nuclear weapon states undertake to conclude agreements (either individually or together with other states) with the IAEA to be in accordance with the agency's statute and safeguards system.

There are skeptics about the assurances provided by the treaty in general, and by its safeguards system, in particular. For example, Congressman Craig Hosmer, ranking Republican member of the Joint Committee on Atomic Energy, has taken the position that the Non-Proliferation Treaty would make little difference to the ninety or more countries who are "have nots," and "never can be" nuclear weapon countries, but that the treaty would not succeed in deterring the dozen or so "have nots" who "can be." Congressman Hosmer is particularly skeptical about the mandatory inspection requirement for peaceful nuclear activities of non-nuclear weapon countries. No safeguards system, he claims, certainly not the one in contemplation, could provide assurance that any one of the advanced countries, if bent on diversion to a military program, could not "beat the system" of safeguards without much risk of exposure. He considers the IAEA system, the central verification instrument of the treaty, to be embryonic, incomplete, understaffed, under-financed, and likely to be overwhelmed by the assignment of inspecting all the nuclear facilities of the non-nuclear weapon countries—not to mention those of the United States and the United Kingdom who have volunteered, separately from the treaty, to put their peaceful nuclear facilities under agency safeguards.

The indictment is overstated in its negative appraisal of the IAEA's system and its ability to grow with the job, and to do it effectively. But more fundamentally, the indictment misses the point that goes to the heart of the assurances to be provided by the safeguards system under Article III of the Non-Proliferation Treaty. The purpose of the safeguards system has never been to make it impossible for non-nuclear weapon countries to divert enriched uranium, or to take the plutonium produced by reactors to build bombs. No foreseeable system can *prevent* diversion to military uses; it can only increase the likelihood that diversion will be detected. And even in a detection role, no system, without being impracticably intrusive, can raise the likelihood of detecting diversion close to certainty. The central aim of the safeguards system is to make the likelihood of detection of monkey business sufficiently strong so that any country will think twice about going out to "beat the system." Detection of the secret diversion of fissionable material to build bombs would be very embarrassing for any nation, and that is precisely what the safeguards system aims to accentuate. Article III of the Non-Proliferation Treaty, after all, operates in conjunction with the solemn obligations undertaken by nuclear and non-nuclear weapon powers under Articles I and II, so as to provide more specific assurance that lawful, peaceful nuclear activities remain peaceful. The better the system gets in the future, the longer a non-nuclear weapon party to the treaty will think about the consequences before secretly undertaking to divert fissionable material in inspected facilities. It can under appropriate circumstances withdraw from the treaty by the direct route of the treaty withdrawal clause. But formal action announcing withdrawal would produce international repercussions, and could leave a perilous interval after a withdrawing country declared it would develop and probably test nuclear weapons.

For those who ratify the treaty, nuclear or non-nuclear weapon nations, there are real prospects of assurance that the international inspection system would give significant teeth to the treaty, which it otherwise could not have. A mandatory safeguards system for the non-nuclear weapon countries is recognizably a sticky obstacle to ratification by several key nations, and is by no means foolproof. If set in motion, however, it would constitute a major landmark and genuine innovation in the field of arms control and international law.

There was a large initial jump, perhaps fortunately unapprehended at the time, in the transfer of safeguards under bilateral agreements, such as those of the United States with over thirty nations in its "Atoms for Peace" program launched in 1953, to uniform international (IAEA) system of controls, or, in the case of the six EURATOM countries, in "folding in" bilateral agreements to an effective regional safeguards system. These transfers were successfully accomplished, piecemeal, as each agreement came up for renewal, beginning in the early 1960's.

There will be a much larger jump to a system of mandatory international safeguards to apply to all nuclear facilities of non-nuclear weapon countries that exist or are projected for the 1970's. These safeguards would apply to nuclear activities, whether or not developed with outside assistance that had "safeguards strings" attached to it.

Under the safeguards of the Non-Proliferation Treaty, a ratifying country could no longer "go it alone," using its own uranium, building its own reactors, and producing its own plutonium to build its own bombs, as it chose. If widely adhered to, the treaty, verified by international inspection, would thus increase assurances against the proliferation of nuclear weapons by a new order of magnitude.

Acceptance of Safeguards

By March, 1970, ratification of the Non-Proliferation Treaty by more than the necessary forty nations and by the three signatory nuclear weapon powers was accomplished, and the treaty entered into force. Now that the treaty is in effect the issue of asymmetry is greatly reduced. Pressure on the remaining countries that have not yet ratified will come not just from the nuclear weapon powers, but from large numbers of *non*-nuclear weapon powers who have ratified the treaty.

Nevertheless, the process of securing ratification by remaining key non-nuclear weapon countries will not be a simple one. The ratification of the EURATOM countries will hinge on the successful outcome of the forth-coming negotiations between EURATOM and the IAEA. Compounding the problem is the position taken by some countries, such as Japan, that there should be no discrimination between the IAEA's treatment of regional and national safeguards systems. The obvious fallacy in that position is that a regional group of nations, such as EURATOM, uses the inspection system to keep track of each other, whereas any single nation could establish its own procedures to divert plutonium, covertly, to build bombs whenever it chose. Accordingly, the intrusiveness of inspection needed by the IAEA to verify the fulfillment of obligations under the treaty by a group of nations with its own regional inspection need not be as great as for an individual country with sole control over the national system it has put into effect to assure itself against misuse of nuclear materials.

The complications produced by a mandatory IAEA safeguards system are genuine, however, and the assurances provided by the treaty will be seriously reduced if there is refusal to ratify, or even if there is a prolonged delay in ratification, by a number of the more advanced countries. This could lead some countries who have already ratified to reconsider, and perhaps withdraw from the treaty, because their potential adversaries have continued to refuse to ratify it.

The offer by the United States and the United Kingdom to accept IAEA inspection on their own peaceful facilities, separately from their obligations under the treaty, has proved valuable in lowering the tone of the arguments, and in reducing the sense of discrimination between nuclear and non-nuclear weapon countries. The offer demonstrated that if there were inconveniences, expenses, and competitive disadvantages in international inspection, they will be assumed by at least two of the signatory nuclear weapon powers.

Applicability of Safeguards

If the hurdles to ratification can be surmounted, further uncertainties will remain about safeguards. There are limits to the reach of the verification system, and the assurances provided by the treaty's safeguards. There is no verification of the undertaking by the parties, under Articles I and II, not to transfer or receive or manufacture nuclear weapons. Nor are there any safeguards under Article III to insure that a non-nuclear weapon state does not establish a secret nuclear weapons program entirely outside and independent of its peaceful nuclear industry. Such conduct would constitute a violation of Articles I or II of the treaty, but would not be uncovered by the IAEA inspection system of "declared" peaceful facilities under Article III. From its inception, the IAEA has not operated as an intelligence agency and there is no provision for agency inspectors to look for undeclared facilities, or to inspect them when there is evidence, independently provided, of clandestine nuclear weapons facilities. This contrasts with the treaty of Tlatelolco (Treaty for the Prohibition of Nuclear Weapons in Latin America), which does contain provision for special inspection, where prohibited activity is suspected or charged, by a council of the members of that treaty.

There is further ambiguity about the reach of the inspection provisions of Article III. Although the IAEA's own statute provides safeguards to insure that materials and equipment are not used to further "any military purpose," the treaty is concerned with diversion specifically to manufacture nuclear weapons or other nuclear explosives. For example, the treaty is silent about diversion of material not to manufacture weapons, but for use in a military production program of weapons-grade plutonium, or in a nuclear submarine propulsion program. Furthermore, Article III does not seem to require safeguards on imports into a non-weapon state for such military (but not specifically weapons) activities.

Sanctions

Finally, there are no sanctions for violations in the Non-Proliferation Treaty, although there are sanctions provided in the IAEA's own statute (Article XII C) for violations of the agency's existing safeguards agreements. This is obviously a problem to be solved in the course of individual negotiations under the Non-Proliferation Treaty with the ratifying countries. From the treaty standpoint, there are two significant sanctions under the current IAEA agreements. First, the IAEA inspectors are to report any "non-compliance" with its safeguards agreement to the agency's Director General, who then reports it to the Board of Governors. The board reports it to the members of the agency, and to the Security Council and General Assembly of the United Nations. Then, secondly, if the country does not take "corrective action," the agency may recall materials and equipment, and suspend the country from the rights and privileges of membership in the IAEA.

The ambiguities about the application of agency sanctions under the Non-Proliferation Treaty may prove largely academic, or they may further complicate negotiations of safeguards agreement under the treaty. Probably more decisive than any threat of sanctions will be the threat of detection of a treaty violation. (If detected, the country would probably take the opportunity to withdraw from the treaty, in its supreme national interest, with or without the treaty's prescribed three months' advance notice.) The main point is the one we began with. Safeguards under the treaty will be effective primarily because nations do not like to run the risk of being caught cheating.

8 Plowshare Evaluation

David B. Brooks
Henry R. Myers

The development of nuclear weapons followed from a recognition of the military value of being able to increase enormously the explosive power that could be rained upon an enemy. The practical feasibility of nuclear explosives suggested they might be used in projects with economic objectives. This possibility is being actively investigated by the United States in its Plowshare Program and by the Soviet Union. To date the United States has spent approximately $115 million on its program. Many other nations have expressed an interest or are themselves conducting technical analyses of applications that might benefit them.

Applications under consideration include the employment of nuclear explosions

...to assist in the recovery of natural resources
...to create cavities for the storage of natural gas
...to aid in water resources development
...to excavate canals and harbors
...to change the course of rivers and construct dams
...to be a radiation source in scientific experiments.

Thus far, most of the U. S. effort has been directed at developing excavation technology. This emphasis has been criticized on grounds that the greatest potential is in resource extraction and gas storage and that, therefore, these applications should receive a greater fraction of the research and development effort.

The per-kiloton costs associated with the use of nuclear explosives decrease as the total yield increases. Therefore, the greatest potential savings are expected in very large projects that require large detonations. The value of such projects can be assessed only with great difficulty. Associated non-economic problems are most difficult to surmount. In those situations where explosive yields are relatively low, and where economic calculations are more tractable, prospective economic gains, to the extent that they exist, are not as great.

Since the technology does not seem to possess overwhelming and obvious advantages, estimates of its economic utility depend upon conclusions drawn from usually ambiguous analyses. Economic calculations are complicated by lack of data and the presence of a large number of intangible factors. Moreover, there may be overriding political considerations that determine whether or not certain possibilities are developed and exercised.

The following discussion addresses the general problem of determining economic utility as well as the prognosis of specific Plowshare applications.[1] The economic utility of the nuclear technique depends upon a cost-benefit comparison between the nuclear technique and other means of achieving the same end.

In those situations where the nuclear method has an economic advantage, it is necessary to establish the existence of two conditions. First, the expected benefits must exceed the cost. Second, the return on the investment should be greater than the return from an equivalent investment in other projects whose object may or may not be the same end.

The General Problem

Unfortunately, it is not possible to reach definitive conclusions concerning economic utility; i.e., it is not possible to make meaningful statements to the effect that an investment of $X has a Y percent probability of yielding a return of Z, etc. In all cases cost-benefit analyses are dominated by imponderables of the following kinds:

1. *Unknowns that might be resolved through relatively modest experiment.* In all proposed applications, estimates of economic utility depend upon analysis of data that can be obtained through experiments. While some experiments have been conducted, there is still insufficient data to make it possible to answer outstanding questions.

2. *Unknowns that cannot be resolved through relatively modest experiment.* In some cases it will be necessary to carry out the project itself to determine whether it was economically advantageous or even technically feasible. This would be the situation where it was necessary to detonate very large devices in projects that were unique, such as in the excavation of a sea-level Panama Canal.

3. *Unknowns that depend upon developments in other technologies.* The

economic utility of a specific application will always depend upon the costs and benefits associated with non-nuclear techniques. Since such techniques are continually under development, it is necessary to make intrinsically imprecise estimates of what developments might occur in the competing technology.

4. *Uncertainties that depend upon the stringency of safety precautions.* The cost of using nuclear explosives will be sensitive to the level of safety that is required. Costs associated with safety measures cannot be determined until specific projects are proposed and considered by the appropriate authorities. This may be true not only because of the direct cost of safety measures, but also because explosives may have to be produced below the optimum size to avoid seismic and air-blast effects.

5. *The extent to which costs associated with research and development must be assigned to a particular application.* In the United States (and probably the Soviet Union) a large part of the development and production costs are charged to the weapons program. Where the line is drawn on this will affect significantly the economic calculations. In addition, if governments underwrite the costs associated with the development of a specific application, this will also influence the economics of that application for industrial use.

6. *In projects that could be carried out only with nuclear explosives, it is necessary to decide whether the benefits are as great as if the expenditure of resources had been directed at a different type of project.* Since this involves a comparison of projects of very different kinds, conclusions will not be clear-cut.

7. *The costs and benefits associated with less tangible aspects, such as the social costs of relocating population, the benefits of achieving an unforeseen technological or economic breakthrough, the costs resulting from interference with the ecology or destruction of aesthetic values, etc.* There are no completely satisfactory means of assigning values to these parameters, even though they may be very important.

8. *The costs and benefits associated with political constraints.* These may be very large, but they too are non-quantifiable. Two types of political constraints are significant:

The first results from safety criteria that are based on a margin of safety which is much higher than that applied to other activities sanctioned by the society. In this case the decision might be made that the society will forgo benefits (and hence incur costs) in order to avoid even a small risk of very great damage.

The second type of political constraint relates to arms control. The argument is made that the utilization of nuclear explosives in civil projects enhances the likelihood that weapons technology will spread. In this view, the price paid for *not* developing non-military uses is small if proliferation is made substantially less likely. The converse is also argued: that the Non-Proliferation Treaty provides that the nuclear powers will make the benefits of non-military nuclear technology available to nations that have pledged not to develop nuclear weapons. If now the nuclear powers do not develop the technology, the non-nuclear powers may have an incentive or excuse to develop their own nuclear capabilities.

Furthermore, the Limited Test Ban Treaty restricts development and application of the cratering technology by prohibiting projects that cause radioactivity to escape borders of the nation in which the detonation occurs. The argument concerning the meaning of what constitutes the presence of debris hinges upon the assumed costs and benefits associated with various interpretations. A strict interpretation emphasizes the value of arms control. A weak one emphasizes the value of nuclear excavation.

9. *Possible costs resulting from a catastrophic accident.* While such an accident may be unlikely, the costs associated with it would be very high. The probability of such an accident and the magnitude of its associated costs are both very difficult to estimate.

The preceding imponderables will, as far as each application is concerned, tend to dominate any conclusion concerning the economic utility of a specific application. To the extent that they can be expressed, they tend to reduce the benefits and increase the costs in any specific application.[2] Therefore, conclusions as to what might or might not be economic will, at this time, be determined by subjective judgments that reflect the biases of those who make them.

Specific Applications

The decision to expend resources on the development of a particular application must depend upon an evaluation of the likelihood that the technique will, if developed, offer economic advantage. It will also depend upon the magnitude of that advantage and the expected return from expenditures in other areas.

The *a priori* likelihood of success necessary to justify a Plowsharelike research and development effort will have to be higher for nations that have not developed nuclear weapons than for those which have. This follows from the fact that in the course of developing and producing nuclear weapons, a substantial portion of the non-military technology is achieved as a by-product. It appears very unlikely that the economic advantage to be derived from the use of nuclear explosives will be sufficient to justify an explosives development program other than one whose principal objective is to achieve a nuclear weapons capability.

In the following section, several applications are considered in sufficient detail to present an idea of whether that application will be of practical significance in the next several decades. The first part of the discussion is limited to what appear to be the most promising applications, which are discussed in the open literature in the United States. A later section focuses on interests and activities of the Soviet Union.

Stimulation of Gas Flow

There are large gas reservoirs that are not economical to exploit because the gas is trapped in low-permeability rock. Gas flow from such reservoirs might be substantially increased by detonation of a nuclear device, which would create a large zone of cracks and rubble through which the gas could move with relative ease.

At the present time, annual gas consumption in the United States is approximately 20 trillion cubic feet per year and is increasing at a rate of approximately one trillion cubic feet per year. One 50 kiloton nuclear detonation might be expected to stimulate the production of about 0.001 trillion cubic feet per year for 20 years. About one thousand 50-kiloton explosions would be required to stimulate one trillion cubic feet per year, which is approximately 5 percent of present consumption in the United States.

Whether the technique makes it worthwhile to extract gas from currently uneconomical deposits depends upon the cost of nuclear devices, emplacement and detonation costs, and the cost of removing radioactive products from the gas that is produced. These costs must be compared with those incurred in more conventional procedures employed in the case of tight deposits; e.g., drilling more closely spaced wells, hydraulic fracturing, and the use of chemical explosives.

In addition, economic feasibility depends upon the cost of energy obtained from nuclear-stimulated gas as compared with the cost of energy obtained from other sources.

Nuclear stimulation projects have attracted substantial investment by commercial gas producers. Two experiments have been conducted and others are in the planning stage. The fact that commercial gas producers have been willing to invest in experimental research on the gas-stimulation technique is cited as an indication of there being good reason to believe that the process will be economically viable. Others point out that the significance of private investment should not be overrated. Risk-taking is normal to gas producers, and in this case the potential return is very large compared with the private cost of experimental projects.

The first experiment on nuclear stimulation is called Gasbuggy. It is being conducted in northwestern New Mexico, where a 26-kiloton nuclear device was detonated at a depth of 4,240 feet on December 10, 1967. Current indications are that long-term gas production rates will be increased eight-fold with respect to nearby unstimulated wells. This compares to pre-shot predictions of a threefold to sevenfold increase.[3] While this experiment did not demonstrate commercial feasibility of the process (nor was it intended to do so), it did prove that a substantial stimulation of gas flow could be achieved. A continuing analysis will provide useful data on costs and radiation problems.

A second stimulation experiment is Rulison. In this case, a 40-kiloton device was detonated at a depth of 8,427 feet in western Colorado in September, 1969. The cost of the project is estimated at $6.5 million, of which the Austral Oil Company is paying about $6 million.[4] It is too early to infer anything about the economic implication of the results.

Based on experience to date, one expert has concluded that "costs of nuclear stimulation must be drastically reduced for a commercial process."[5] A further indication of the prognosis is contained in the September, 1969, Federal Power Commission staff report on National Gas Supply and Demand. In its discussion of the source of future gas supplies, the staff did not consider that nuclear stimulation was one of the more promising gas sources for the period beyond 1973 and during the 1980's. This study concluded:

> However, based on present knowledge it is impossible to predict the magnitude, timing and cost of gas that may be released by this technique or the possible impact the additional reserves would have on the future national gas supply. In addition, important economic and social considerations must be resolved before such techniques experience large-scale commercial use. We do not anticipate that nuclear stimulation techniques will have a measurable effect on domestic supply availability in the foreseeable future.

This conclusion was based in part on a belief that there were also political and long-range environmental consequences to be considered. Thus, it was noted that:

> In order to substantially increase natural gas availability, however, thousands of nuclear devices will have to be detonated. In view of the increasingly forceful and articulate expressions of concern being voiced for the integrity of the environment, such large-scale application might not gain public acceptance.

Gasbuggy, Rulison, and follow-on experiments will together provide reasonably definitive information on the costs of gas obtained through gas stimulation. These costs will include expenses associated with procurement of the device, drilling, detonation, reduction of radioactivity to acceptable levels, and interest charges. This cost information, when combined with relevant data concerning conventional stimulation and other energy sources, will make it possible to estimate the net economic gain. Large-scale implementation of nuclear gas stimulation will then depend on a favorable judgment of the economics, a determination that the adverse environmental effects are acceptable, and public acceptance.

Gas Storage in Nuclear Rubble Cavities

High-pressure pipelines transport most natural gas from areas in which it is produced to consumer markets. In order to maximize the return on the considerable investment in transportaiton facilities, it is necessary to operate them as near to capacity as possible during the entire year. Consumption is higher in winter than in summer, and it is therefore desirable to store gas in market areas during that part of the year when demand is low.

The least expensive gas-storage facilities (and the ones most widely used at the present time) are depleted gas fields and certain types of aquifers. But the storage capacity of these is said to be insufficient to meet even the current demand at present gas prices. That is, if additional storage capacity could be obtained at the same operating cost as current facilities, additional space could be used immediately. Some estimates (e.g., Ketch proposal) suggest the demand for storage in 1975 will be about three times the present capacity. In assessing the real utility of additional storage volume, it is necessary to determine the magnitude of the demand as a function of the cost.

One means of increasing gas-storage capacity is the construction of facilities to store the gas in liquid form. This procedure, however, appears to be considerably more expensive than is the use of depleted gas fields and may be useful only for meeting demand on the coldest days. Another technique under investigation is storage in rubble cavities produced by nuclear explosions. The cost of storage in nuclear cavities for yields less than 50 kilotons is estimated to be intermediate between that of storage in depleted gas fields and that of storage in the liquid form. For nuclear yields above 50 kilotons, costs are estimated to be roughly equivalent to those of depleted gas fields.

A consideration of the details leads to the conclusion that the situation is very complex. Predictions of need require estimates concerning future developments in many areas of technology such as nuclear power production, coal gassification, gas liquefication, stimulation of gas flow by nuclear explosions, extraction of oil from shale, and perhaps others. Moreover, gas storage requirements will be related to the future distribution of gas production areas, the intensity of exploration activity, the price of imports, and the patterns of gas usage.

Cost-benefit analyses are further complicated by intangibles associated with the detonation of nuclear explosives. Most important is the problem of gaining public acceptance.

If a substantial fraction of estimated new storage capacity requirements (i.e., about 25 percent) are to be met by creating nuclear rubble cavities, it will be necessary to detonate on the order of 1,000 devices in the 25 to 100 kiloton range.[6] Project Ketch, which was to be a test of the technique, was not authorized because of citizen concern over safety. Increasing citizen involvement in environmental matters (as in the case of gas stimulation) suggests that it is unlikely that any significant number of storage projects will be allowed at sites that are in close proximity to market areas. The implication of this is difficult to predict in the absence of more complete knowledge of the restrictions that might be imposed.

As is the situation with other applications, from the public's perspective, the economics of gas storage in nuclear rubble cavities depends in large part upon intangible factors that are largely unrelated to the costs associated with creating cavities. From the perspective of specific companies involved in the transmission and distribution of natural gas, the situation is probably less complex and the prognosis more sanguine. This is particularly true if a large fraction of the costs associated with developing suitable nuclear explosives is borne by the Atomic Energy Commission.

Production of Oil from Shale

Exceedingly large energy reserves are contained in oil shales, which at this time are uneconomical to exploit. Economic extraction of oil from shale is the objective of a substantial research program in the United States. One possibility that is being considered involves the underground detonation of nuclear explosives to create a zone of rubblized shale. Air is forced into the rubble zone and the shale-air mixture is ignited. This heats the shale and causes the separation of the oil from it. The oil flows to the bottom of the cavity and is then extracted.

In 1967, fifteen oil and related companies proposed to the Atomic Energy Commission and the Department of the Interior an experiment called Bronco. The objective was to obtain data that might provide a better understanding of the potential of the process. The government agencies and industrial organizations have not yet agreed on terms of the contract under which the experiment would be conducted.

The economic feasibility of this process depends in part upon the values of parameters that may be experimentally determined, such as pressure at which air must be forced into the cavity and the percent of oil recovered from the shale. The greatest uncertainties revolve about retorting and extracting the oil, rather than the detonation of the nuclear explosive. The economics are also strongly affected by the overall level of oil reserves. The economic utility of the process appears to be largely determined by the price of oil from other sources, including imported oil. The more scarce such oil becomes, the more attractive will be production of oil from shale. Recently, the Atomic Energy Commission has indicated that the discovery of oil in northern Alaska has resulted in a diminished interest in oil from shale.[7]

The Use of Nuclear Explosives to Assist in the Recovery of Copper

Depletion of high-grade copper ore bodies makes it desirable to develop more economical procedures for exploiting low-grade deposits. One possibility is to use nuclear explosions to create rubble cavities in ore bodies. Acid is then passed through the fractured ore. The copper goes into solution, which is extracted as it collects in a pool at the bottom of the cavity. This is called in-situ leaching. Project Sloop has been proposed by the Atomic Energy Commission, the Bureau of Mines, and the Kennecott Copper Company as an experiment to determine the feasibility of the process.

In order that the chemical reaction between the acid and the ore proceed efficiently, it is necessary that the rubble particles be of sufficiently small dimensions. Therefore, a particularly important characteristic that needs to be determined is the presently unknown distribution of particle sizes in the rubble cavity.

An economic analysis accompanying the Sloop proposal[8] suggests that the process would be economical if applied to a 240-million-ton leaching reserve created by approximately forty 100-kiloton detonations. Since the author of the proposal did not provide the cost parameters upon which his conclusion was based, it is not possible to compare the price of copper obtained in this manner with present prices. The Sloop proposal did not discuss costs associated with radioactive contamination or seismic damage. However, a study conducted under the auspices of the Oak Ridge National Laboratory suggests that radioactivity would not be a significant problem. Seismic damage would depend upon the proximity of the project to vulnerable structures.

A November, 1967, Bureau of Mines report (R16996) presents a prognosis that may properly reflect awareness of both the potential and the problems associated with implementation:

> Present information indicates that a copper deposit can be safely fractured with a nuclear explosive and the copper successfully re-

covered by the in-situ leaching method. The process is not yet at the stage where it can be presented to the mining industry as a technique proven in all its aspects, but it is a method with high success potential. Unknown factors must be evaluated by a full-scale test before the economics or the extent of the use of the method by the mining industry can be predicted.

Preliminary calculations indicate that the cost of fracturing a copper deposit with nuclear explosives may range from 12.8 to 55.2 cents per ton or in some cases less than a cent per pound of recoverable copper. Copper may be recovered at less cost than by conventional methods. Deposits with 4 pounds of recoverable copper per ton of ore may be economic and production from a deposit may begin in less than half the time required for conventional methods.

Nuclear Excavation

The most spectacular economic application of nuclear explosives is earth moving or excavation. In this case, the nuclear explosion breaks up the rock and soil and ejects it from the excavation. Nuclear explosions might then be used as an aid in the construction of canals, harbors, dams, or highways. The projects in which nuclear excavations might be most advantageous are those that are very large and unique. That is, unlike the resource extraction applications where many explosions of low or moderate yield might be required, each excavation will require relatively few explosions of very high yield.

Each excavation application will tend to differ markedly from others and, therefore, it will be much more difficult to extrapolate the results from one project or experiment to another as may be done in underground engineering. Even when the direct effects of the blast can be predicted with fair accuracy, the side effects that depend upon local conditions will always introduce additional elements of uncertainty. The large scale and unique character insure that the results of economic analyses will be ambiguous.

Benefits and costs associated with large projects are difficult to assess even when conventional procedures are employed. It is not unlikely that there will be unforeseen consequences whose associated costs or benefits are large enough to determine the net worth of the project. For example, the Aswan Dam will very substantially alter the flow of the Nile River and eliminate the floods that periodically replenish the soils in the Nile Delta. If the capability of the Delta soils to produce food were thereby diminished, the benefits of irrigation made possible by the dam might be negated. Large-scale projects that have been proposed to alter the course of rivers or to irrigate deserts may bring about ecological changes whose nature cannot be predicted.

Were there no need for concern with either radiation safety, air blast, or ground shock, it would be clearly more economical to use nuclear explosives than conventional means, providing the explosive power to be concentrated at one point exceeds about 1,000 tons of chemical explosive equivalent. Because in all cases it will be necessary to consider these safety factors, the minimum distance of excavation projects from populated areas (or, alternatively, the maximum yield device that can be detonated) is determined by the sensitivity of structure to earth shock and air blast and the extent to which radioactive fallout can be adequately minimized.

The adverse side effects of excavation explosions can be reduced or eliminated, although this will increase costs. Through development and production of low-fission explosives, radiation can probably be reduced to the point where the dominant safety concern is air blast and earth shock. In any event, for excavation applications, the costs associated with safety are considerable. Moreover, there exists the very real possibility that projects will not be conducted as a result of the inability to provide sufficient assurance that the hazards have been minimized.

In order to estimate costs, it is necessary to have data concerning the physical characteristics of craters and the air blast, ground shock, and fallout caused by the detonation. Experiments conducted thus far indicate that the cratering mechanism functions approximately as had been predicted. There are, however, important questions to be resolved and the answers will markedly affect cost estimates.

Experiments that are now part of the Plowshare plan include Project Yawl (several hundred Kilotons in hard rock), Project Galley (a row-charge experiment consisting of five to seven explosives with yields ranging "from a few tons to a few hundreds of Kilotons to excavate a linear crater through uneven terrain"), and Project Gondola (unspecified yield in weak wet rock found on a portion of at least one of the routes proposed for the sea-level Panama Canal). These tests should provide important information with regard to the relationship of yield to crater depth and width at high yields, the dependence of crater size on soil properties, the relationship between slope stability and soil type, the interaction of large row detonations, and the extent to which seismic effects, air blast, and radioactivity can be minimized.

The sea-level Isthmian canal is the project that has been most extensively examined as a candidate for nuclear excavation. As such, it can illustrate the difficulties associated with analyses of the economic utility of nuclear cratering. In order to put the problem in perspective, it might be noted that nuclear excavation is expected to cost approximately $0.7 billion and conventional excavation of a sea-level canal about $2 billion. But even these costs do not adequately reflect a large number of intangible factors.

The need for a sea-level canal (and hence the value of the benefits associated with it) is itself a subject of controversy. One school of experts believes that the present canal can be appropriately modified with the implementation of the so-called Terminal Lakes Plan. This plan would involve less expense than a sea-level canal constructed by conventional or nuclear means. A canal modified according to the Terminal Lakes Plan would, according to its proponents, be as or more suitable in terms of capacity, ease of operation, safety of transit, and operational costs than a sea-level route. With regard to protection against attack, a modified lock canal is considered by many to be no more vulnerable than a sea-level canal. One argument against the Terminal Lakes Plan is that it might not permit the passage of the largest ships. But the fact that such ships have already been constructed with the knowledge that an Isthmian passage would be denied them for the indefinite future raises the question of the absolute need of any kind of canal for the kinds of cargo carried by very large ships. Moreover, it is not clear that ship-operating costs and sea-level canal tolls will not be such that ship operators would find it more profitable to send their vessels around South America.

But even assuming that analyses indicate that a sea-level canal should be built, there are many subjective factors that enter into cost comparisons between nuclear and conventional construction. Construction by conventional means would allow much more extensive participation by local workers and would lead to the development of skills that would be of great value once the project was completed. Since nuclear excavation would occur along a route different from the present one, the Panamanian economy would be severely affected.

Uncertainties associated with the nuclear excavation process compound the difficulty of making meaningful cost comparisons. While conventional construction would involve techniques that are quite well understood, very little is known about excavation by nuclear explosives. Current estimates suggest that nuclear excavation would require the detonation of hundreds of nuclear devices with a cumulative yield measured in hundreds of megatons. The yield of the largest single detonation of a row of explosive charges is estimated to be 35 megatons. Experiments are necessary to determine the extent to which these yield estimates are meaningful. Recent Atomic Energy Commission testimony suggests that lesser yields may create the desired effects. While the costs of nuclear explosives would not be seriously affected by increasing the average yield, costs associated with safety would increase greatly. It is also possible that the necessary yields, even by the lowest estimates, are so high that the required authorization will never be attained.

Another source of uncertainty revolves around the question of whether the slopes of the excavation will be stable. Experiments planned for the western United States are intended to shed some light on this question. However, it is not clear how applicable the results will be in Panama, where annual rainfall in places is hundreds of inches. Slope instability problems can, in principle, be avoided by using higher yields to create an excavation whose initial dimensions are greater than need be. The slope could then be allowed to reach a stable configuration without filling in the canal. Since high yields may already be a significant obstacle, it would be preferable not to have to resort to this solution. If slope instability problems had to be overcome through conventional construction, the cost would be very high. This could eliminate any advantage offered by the nuclear technique.

In 1965, President Lyndon B. Johnson appointed a commission to conduct a study for the purpose of determining feasibility and the most suitable site for a sea-level canal. The canal study commission's report is to be submitted on December 1, 1970. Few of the uncertainties discussed here should be resolved therein especially in view of President Richard Nixon's decision to request no funds for nuclear excavation experiments in the Fiscal Year 1971 budget. It is likely that in the end whatever choice is made will be determined more by political than economic and technical factors.

Non-Military Applications of Nuclear Explosives in the Soviet Union

The Soviet Union supports a program with objectives and activities similar to those of U.S. Plowshare program. In April 1969, representatives of the United States and Soviet Union attended a meeting in Vienna the purpose of which was to consider the technical status of various possible economic applications of nuclear explosives. There was agreement on the nature of possible applications. A joint statement issued at the conclusion of the meeting stated:

> The parties were of the view that underground nuclear explosions may be successfully used in the not-so-far-off future to stimulate oil and gas production and to create underground cavities. It may also be technically feasible to use them in earth-moving work for the constructing of water reservoirs in arid areas, to dig canals, and in removing the upper layer in surface mining, etc.
>
> Although the economics will vary from project to project, the use of nuclear explosion for those purposes is promising and would permit operations under conditions where conventional methods are either impossible or impracticable.[9]

This statement presumably reflects the official position of the Soviet government as it does of the United States government. A 1969 review of possible applications published in the Soviet Union indicates the thrust of the Soviet effort.[10] This report expresses interest in excavation applications, stimulation of oil and gas flow from non-porous formations, the creation of underground storage facilities, and the use of explosions to fracture ore.

There is also reference to the use of nuclear explosions to control pressure in mines and elsewhere, including the control of gas and oil gushers. (This is an application not discussed in the U.S. literature and, in fact, it is not discussed beyond its being mentioned in the Soviet report.)

The report agrees with the view of American experts that the greatest economic advantage is likely to be achieved in large excavation projects. At the same time, it notes that more emphasis had been given underground explosions that do not cause surface effects in view of "strict adherence" of the Soviet Union to the Limited Nuclear Test Ban Treaty. (Since this treaty came into effect, detectable quantities of radioactive debris from explosions detonated by both the United States and the Soviet Union have crossed national borders. The meaning of debris being "present" is disputed as is the scrupulousness with which the treaty has been observed in this regard.)

The Soviet review indicates substantial cost savings for some applications. The basis for such estimates is not disclosed. As in the case with estimates that appear in U.S. literature, the Soviet estimates presumably are based on subjective evaluations of many intangible factors. The joint statement signed by the Soviet representatives at the Vienna meeting was more restrained (i.e., the emphasis was more on technical than on economic feasibility and nowhere indicated that economic utility had been established for any application).

Conclusion

The preceding discussion indicates the degree to which intangible factors dominate any analysis of the economic utility of nuclear explosives. Any such analysis is, therefore, likely to reflect the perspectives of the analyst.

Statements made by persons associated with the U.S. Atomic Energy Commission, its contractors, and industries involved in non-military applications of nuclear explosives (and their equivalents in other nations) tend to be sanguine about the prospects. Persons whose dominant interest is arms control and the non-proliferation of nuclear weapons tend to give more emphasis to the factors indicating that the economic utility will not be substantial. Those who are concerned with the preservation of the environment weigh heavily the possible costs associated with various polluting effects. Interestingly, the advocates of nuclear explosives believe that certain applications will result in an improvement in environmental quality. In specific cases, the proponents of a technology or procedure competing with one that makes use of nuclear explosives will be more pessimistic in their evaluations of the nuclear means.

In spite of the non-specific nature of the situation, and in part because of it, the following inferences are drawn:

1. Experiments conducted by the United States and the Soviet Union have demonstrated that nuclear explosions can be used to bring about certain desired effects.

2. On the basis of the U.S. experience to date, it appears that in the next several decades the availability of nuclear explosives will not be a key factor in solutions to the major problems confronting mankind. This does not rule out the possibility that there may be aspects of the technology whose exploitation could lead to substantial returns on investment by nations or corporations. For example, if gas obtained through nuclear stimulation were 10 percent less costly than gas obtained through the use of competing techniques, a substantial profit might accrue to investors in the nuclear technique. On the other hand, the 10 percent price differential is unlikely to lead to significant benefits for a large number of people.

3. The economic utility of nuclear explosives has not been established for any of the proposed applications discussed in the available literature.

4. At this time it is not possible to estimate when (if ever) and in what application the use of nuclear explosives will be economically significant.

5. The economic prognosis is very sensitive to the details of the analysis and in particular depends upon the relative weights assigned to many intangible factors.

6. The greatest economic benefit would be achieved in very large projects where costs associated with conventional techniques are prohibitively high. However, the benefits associated with such projects are very difficult to evaluate as are the costs associated with possible unwanted side effects.

7. At this time, gas stimulation and gas storage are the applications that show the most promise.

8. The economic prognosis would be much more pessimistic if a very large portion of the research and development costs and the capital investment in fissionable materials production and fabrication facilities had not been charged off to a weapons development program. From this it follows that nuclear explosives development that is not part of a nuclear weapons program can almost certainly not be justified on economic grounds.

9. In most cases where there might be economic advantages, political and social considerations may prevent the exploitation of the technology.

10. Since there may be unexpected benefits, either in the results of experiments that have already been conceived or in applications that have not heretofore been considered, research in certain areas can be justified by those nations that have already developed nuclear explosives.

9   Plowshare Control

Bernhard G. Bechhoefer

While the term "Plowshare" technically describes only the program sponsored by the U.S. Atomic Energy Commission for "the development of peaceful uses of nuclear explosives,"[1] for convenience in terminology the term is extended to cover any peaceful uses of nuclear explosives regardless of the national or international source of the program.[2]

Article V of the Non-Proliferation Treaty[3] contemplates "a special international agreement or agreements" establishing "an appropriate international body with adequate representation of non-nuclear-weapon States" to deal with a variety of problems related to such states' obtaining benefits from peaceful applications of nuclear explosions. Such an international body would be responsible for "appropriate international observation" and for developing "appropriate international procedures." Thus it might have full, partial, or minimal responsibility for the control measures required to assure that the peaceful explosion programs do not lead to nuclear proliferation.

Article V provides for negotiations on this subject to commence as soon as possible after the treaty has entered into force. However, the UN General Assembly figuratively speaking "jumped the gun" and called for its Secretary General to prepare a report on the general subject in consultation with the members of the United Nations, even before the treaty entered into force.[4] The materials submitted pursuant to the General Assembly's resolution apparently resulted in considerable international consensus as to the nature both of the international body that is likely to be formed pursuant to Article V of the Non-Proliferation Treaty and of the extent and nature of international observation.

Therefore, in this chapter we shall first describe the resources available for international control, including the probable characteristics of such an international body and the functions it is practically certain to perform. We shall then consider whether the available international resources for control are suitable or adequate to perform the necessary control measures to prevent nuclear proliferation.

International Resources for Plowshare

The IAEA

It seems clear, particularly after the Conference of Non-Nuclear-Weapon States, that the IAEA itself will be the international body that will undertake the tasks contemplated in Article V relating to international use of peaceful nuclear explosions. The General Assembly Resolution called for the establishment of an international service for peaceful nuclear explosions *within the framework of the IAEA*. However, the three nuclear power signatories to the treaty (the United States, United Kingdom and Soviet Union) were unanimous in the view that the IAEA should utilize its existing organization for that purpose.[5]

The strongest opposition to using the IAEA as the international body came from Mexico, which submitted a detailed and abrasive alternative suggestion.[6] The Mexican objection to the use of IAEA in essence rested on contentions that the nuclear weapon states have too great control over IAEA decisions under the voting formula provided in the IAEA charter; states not adhering to the Non-Proliferation Treaty (in particular, states adhering to the Treaty for Prohibition of Nuclear Weapons in Latin America) should be permitted to benefit from peaceful nuclear explosions; and the international body should have authority far in excess of that contemplated in Article V, particularly the power to compel the nuclear weapon states to furnish the services to the non-nuclear weapon states.[7]

Since all of these suggestions move in the direction of enhancing the powers of the international body in a manner that in some instances would be contrary to the Non-Proliferation Treaty and in all instances would be objectionable to the nuclear weapon states, it may be assumed that the IAEA will be the international organ to implement Article V.

Functions of IAEA Relating to International Plowshare
Other Than Observation

In order to gauge the capability of the IAEA to perform the observation functions under Article V of the treaty, some consideration of total functions of IAEA concerning peaceful explosions seem relevant. The

Secretary General compiled a detailed list of relatively non-controversial functions that the IAEA could perform in the use of nuclear explosives.[8] In highly abbreviated form these functions are:

1. Information exchange.

2. Services to requesting member states, such as economic and safety reviews, technological assistance, feasibility study arrangements, and intermediary arrangements (intermediary between the weapon states and the non-weapon states desiring the peaceful explosion services).

3. Access to scientific by-products.[9]

The United States, United Kingdom, and Soviet Union all contemplate that the IAEA should perform such functions.

A more controversial function, not directly associated with observation, would be "the crucial 'go ahead' decision" authorizing the peaceful explosion.[10] The text of Article V makes it clear that the non-nuclear weapon states will obtain the benefits "through a special international agreement or agreements through an appropriate international body." The comments of the Soviet Union likewise make clear its position that the "go ahead" decision will be made by agreement between a non-nuclear weapon state and a weapon state, and that the international body will merely be an intermediary.[11] Article V of the treaty specifically permits peaceful explosions under bilateral agreements between the weapon states and the non-weapon states, without the international body playing any role at all—even that of intermediary.

At the other extreme, the Mexican proposal[12] contemplates a special fund at the disposal of the international body, which would be set up as a result of pledges made at two-year intervals by both weapon and non-weapon states. The international body would be in a position to authorize the particular peaceful explosion and allocate funds to take care of the obligations of the non-weapon state. Thus, the Mexican proposal goes as far as possible—probably beyond treaty limits—in the direction of a binding "go ahead" decision of an international body. It cannot go the whole distance since even the Mexican proposal recognizes that the costs of the explosions should be determined by agreements between the states directly concerned. Likewise, the international body could not veto the arrangements for an explosion that it had not approved in view of the final sentence of Article V permitting the parties to the treaty to obtain the benefits directly through bilateral agreements.

The United States commented that it "does not anticipate any scarcity of nuclear explosive devices necessary to perform this service once the technology for applying nuclear explosions to peaceful uses reaches a stage of commercial application."[13] This would seem to imply that if the international body gave a "go ahead" signal, it would be possible to work out arrangements for the explosion. Therefore, the IAEA need not set up quotas of peaceful explosions and allocate the quotas among interested states. Likewise, the development of relatively clean explosive devices will avoid the necessity of establishing fallout quotas. (This will be discussed again below.) It is clear that the United States does not consider that a nuclear weapon state would be legally bound to supply the service merely because the project requiring the service had been approved by the international body.[14]

Observation Function of IAEA as to International Plowshare

The section of the report of the Secretary General concerning "appropriate international observation" indicated that this would be a suitable function for the IAEA, but that the concept would require definition and determination of procedures under which the observation would be arranged and carried out.[15] The Soviet Union likewise recognized that the IAEA was suitable to "exercise appropriate international observation over peaceful nuclear explosions" and at the same time emphasized that the explosion of the device would remain under the authority and control of the nuclear weapon state. The United Kingdom and the United States in substance took the same position.[16]

The United States is the only nuclear weapon state that has stated publicly the specific duties the IAEA would perform as a part of its function of international observation. As far back as 1961, the United States and United Kingdom submitted to the Eighteen National Disarmament Committee (ENDC) a Draft Treaty on Discontinuance of Nuclear Weapons Tests containing a detailed statement of a method of international observation of peaceful explosions.[17] While later drafts of such a treaty provide for a similar article to be contained in an annex, none of the later drafts include a specific text.

Since it seems clear that some of the suggestions made in 1961 no longer represent the position of either the United States or United Kingdom, it is preferable to refer to the most recent statement of the U.S. position[18] and then to supplement the recent statements with the more detailed presentation of 1961.

In July, 1968, the Joint Committee on Atomic Energy of the U.S. Congress (JCAE) addressed certain questions to the Atomic Energy Commission concerning international observation of peaceful explosions. The relevant portions of the questions and answers can be summarized as follows:

1. International observers would not be given access to sensitive information regarding the nuclear explosive devices used in an international Plowshare project, since such access would violate Articles I and II of the

Non-Proliferation Treaty. The devices would remain at all times under the custody and control of the nuclear weapon state performing the service.

2. The international observers would be given a reasonable opportunity in an international Plowshare project conducted by the United States to assure that the nuclear explosive devices used "remained under the custody and control of the United States at all times and that the nuclear explosions carried out in the course of furnishing the service were not being used for other than declared purposes."

3. Neither the international observers nor nationals of the recipient non-nuclear weapon state would be permitted access to information concerning the design or internal operation of the nuclear explosive devices.

The 1961 proposals to the ENDC referred to above elaborate in three respects the U.S. position as set forth in the above questions and answers.[19] Two of the elaborations that probably still represent U.S. policy are discussed below. (The third elaboration, which probably no longer is the U.S. position, is considered in the section dealing with reciprocal inspection.)

The draft treaty of 1961 provides that the nuclear weapon state proposing to conduct the explosion submit to the international body responsible for observation (presumably the IAEA) the date, site, and purpose of the detonation; the expected yield of the device; the measures to be taken to ensure against fallout if the explosion is intended to vent; and the measurements to be taken and any experimentation to be conducted in connection with the explosion. This information to be furnished to the international body (which will be described as the "scenario") is a major factor in assuring that the peaceful explosions will result in no military benefits to the nuclear weapon state conducting the explosion.

Under the 1961 proposal, the international body responsible for observation would inspect the device externally; would observe all preparations for and the actual explosion of the device; and would have unlimited access to the vicinity of the explosion to insure that the explosion is carried out as proposed by the nuclear weapon state. Such authority—which seems consistent with the less detailed Atomic Energy Commission presentation in 1968—is also an important factor in insuring the effectiveness of the international observation.

Reciprocal Inspection

The 1961 draft treaty[20] proposed that the nuclear weapon parties "be given an adequate opportunity at a designated inspection site to inspect externally and internally any nuclear device to be detonated . . . and to examine detailed drawings of the device provided that such detailed drawings may not be reproduced or taken away from the inspection site. The device to be detonated shall, after inspection and reassembly, be under the continual surveillance of members of the organization staff until detonation."

This proposal extended to the field of observation of peaceful explosions the principle of "reciprocal inspection"–i.e. the Soviet Union would inspect the United States and vice versa–which has been suggested in other areas of arms control, such as detection of underground nuclear tests and a "freeze" on nuclear delivery vehicles in Central Europe.[21] The rationale for reciprocal inspection in connection with peaceful nuclear detonations is that internal inspection of the device, or even examination of detailed drawings, by an international body might spread the knowledge of weapons technology to nationals of non-weapon states, while reciprocal inspection could not have such a result. During the negotiations of the Limited Nuclear Test Ban Treaty, such a rationale led to discussions not only of reciprocal inspection of explosive devices, but to proposals for joint research programs conducted by the weapon powers to develop devices for peaceful explosions.[22] These discussions assumed the possibility of utilizing for peaceful explosions some of the relatively simple devices developed for the early weapon tests, where presumably the full technology was known to all the nuclear-weapon states.

More recently it has become increasingly apparent that the devices for all peaceful explosions, both underground and those that crater, must be much "cleaner" than the relatively primitive devices used in early weapon tests. The type of "cleanness" for underground explosions will be different from those that vent. Both types of detonations, however, will require sophisticated devices where the United States would be unwilling to communicate the technology to the Soviet Union and vice versa. To quote Ambassador Fisher,[23]

> ... the projects which appear to be of greatest interest–nuclear earth moving projects, such as digging canals or building dams–can be feasible only if highly sophisticated thermo nuclear devices are used. Fission type explosives are not practical for excavation both because the radioactivity release would be unacceptably high and because fissionable material is too costly a source of energy to make such a project economically feasible.

Therefore, at this time, reciprocal inspection as a supplement to international observation would not be feasible. However, it should not be disregarded as a resource for the future when the technology now considered sophisticated becomes routine for all the nuclear weapon states.

Latin American Treaty

The Treaty for the Prohibition of Nuclear Weapons in Latin America[24] calls for a control system to verify "that devices, services, and facilities intended for peaceful uses of nuclear energy are not used in the testing or manufacture of nuclear weapons."[25] The treaty divides the control duties between the IAEA and the council of the "Agency for the Prohibition of Nuclear Weapons in Latin America." The General Secretary of the "agency" and technical personnel designated by the IAEA are given the authority to observe peaceful explosions by Latin American states. Thus, in theory the "agency" is an additional resource. However, the Latin American treaty provisions would violate the Non-Proliferation Treaty if they are construed to authorize peaceful explosions by non-weapon states, except in the remote contingency that some type of peaceful explosion could be devised with no weapon implications. Therefore, for the present the machinery set up by the treaty is merely a potential resource for observation.

The treaty does go into some detail in spelling out the type of observation of peaceful explosions that would be permitted.[26] Of particular interest is Article 18, paragraph 3, which parallels in somewhat more detail recent statements of the U.S. position.

> 3. The General Secretary and the technical personnel designated by the Council and the International Atomic Energy Agency may observe all the preparation, including the explosion of the device, and shall have unrestricted access to any area in the vicinity of the site of the explosion in order to ascertain whether the device and the procedures followed during the explosion are in conformity with the information supplied under paragraph 2 of this article and the other provisions of this Treaty.

Requirements for Safeguards

Three Hypotheses

In dealing with the requirements for safeguards to prevent utilizing peaceful nuclear explosions for weapons development it is necessary to hypothesize three situations that might exist over the next ten to fifteen years. While hypotheses in addition to the three listed below are possible, the analyses of the three situations disclose all substantial problem areas. The three hypothetical situations are:

1. Confining peaceful nuclear explosions to those that do not vent and continuation of the existing Limited Nuclear Test Ban Treaty.

2. Confining peaceful explosions to those that do not vent and amending the Test Ban Treaty to prohibit all nuclear explosions except peaceful explosions.

3. Amending the Test Ban Treaty to permit explosions for peaceful purposes even though the explosions vent and to prohibit all other nuclear explosions.

These are realistic hypotheses since the nuclear weapon states all contemplate amendment of the Limited Nuclear Test Ban Treaty to authorize peaceful explosions.[27]

CONFINING PEACEFUL EXPLOSIONS TO THOSE THAT DO NOT VENT AND CONTINUATION OF THE EXISTING LIMITED NUCLEAR TEST BAN TREATY

It should first be noted that the terminology "confining peaceful explosions to those that do not vent" is not precise. The Test Ban Treaty nowhere uses the term "vent," but prohibits all nuclear explosions in the atmosphere; beyond its limits, including outer space; or under water. It also prohibits explosions in other environments "if such explosions cause radioactive debris to be present outside the territorial limits of the State under whose jurisdiction or control such explosion is conducted." To simplify terminology, the term "vent" is used to describe all underground explosions coming within the prohibition of the Test Ban Treaty, despite the fact that explosions that vent violate the treaty only if the venting causes radioactive debris in measurable quantities outside the territorial limits of the state where the explosion took place.

The existing Test Ban Treaty permits all states to carry out underground nuclear explosions that do not vent, whether they are for peaceful or weapon purposes.[28] The Non-Proliferation Treaty, however, prohibits non-weapon states from exploding any nuclear devices and, therefore, deprives them of their existing right to conduct underground nuclear explosions.

The Soviet Union, the United States, and the United Kingdom have all insisted that they will maintain control over the explosive devices. If one of the weapon states announced that it was conducting a peaceful nuclear explosion for the benefit of a non-weapon state and, in fact, the explosion served a military purpose, there would still be no violation of either the Test Ban Treaty or the Non-Proliferation Treaty unless the weapon state utilized the explosion to instruct the non-weapon state in the technology of nuclear explosions.[29]

Since the explosions will take place outside their territories, the sole purpose of international observation would be to make sure that the weapon state was, in fact, controlling the explosion. The United States has made it completely clear that its interpretation of "appropriate international observation and explosion" would permit the international body to carry on such a function.[30] The Soviet Union apparently has reached the same conclusions through endorsing the concept of "appropriate international observation of the explosion," but its representatives have not elaborated to any great degree the details of international observation as they understand it.[31] The interna-

tional organization required to observe such explosions would be neither large
nor complex. An estimate of personnel required for data recording of routine
nuclear operations is from ten to twenty.[32]

CONFINING PEACEFUL EXPLOSIONS TO THOSE THAT DO NOT VENT AND AMENDMENT OF THE TEST BAN TREATY TO PROHIBIT ALL NUCLEAR EXPLOSIONS EXCEPT PEACEFUL EXPLOSIONS

During the negotiations that resulted in the Limited Nuclear Test Ban
Treaty, the preferred position of both the United States and the Soviet Union
was to have a treaty that prohibited all nuclear explosions in all environments. It was impossible to reach agreement on a comprehensive test ban
between the Soviet Union and the United States, primarily because the Soviet
Union was unwilling to permit limited inspection in its territories to check on
possible violations of a ban on underground nuclear explosions. The Soviet
Union was willing to rely on its national capabilities to determine whether the
United States had violated the treaty, but undoubtedly because of the
existence of the "iron curtain" the United States did not have similar
confidence that its national capabilities would detect all underground nuclear
explosions within the Soviet Union.

Since the adoption of the Limited Test Ban Treaty the chief quest for
further measures to prevent proliferation of nuclear weapons has been routed
in a different direction—the direction that produced the Non-Proliferation
Treaty. However, considerable international support has at all times existed
for revising the Test Ban Treaty so that it would prohibit underground
explosions as well as explosions in other environments.

Despite the complexities involved in reconciling a peaceful explosion
program with comprehensive test ban, it seems probable that at an early stage
in international progress toward arms control, the limited test ban will
become an unlimited test ban for military explosions.[33]

While the nuclear weapon states contemplate amendment of the Limited
Test Ban Treaty to authorize peaceful explosions,[34] they—and particularly
the Soviet Union—are a trifle vague or perhaps coy in indicating the nature
and timing of the amendment. This is understandable since practical applications of Plowshare seem several years away and, therefore, any international
negotiations to amend the treaty seem premature. An amendment of the
treaty to prohibit military explosions but to permit peaceful explosions that
do not vent will raise a number of control questions.

First, it would be necessary for the nuclear weapon state conducting the
explosion to keep full control of the explosive device in order to prevent the
spread of technology to the non-weapon state where the explosion is
conducted. This control problem is the same as the problem described under

the previous hypothesis where there was no change in the Test Ban Treaty. As pointed out in the previous section, the provisions for international observation seem adequate to meet this contingency.

A second problem that does not arise until the Test Ban Treaty becomes a comprehensive ban is the problem that has prevented agreement—detection of underground explosions. It seems probable that in 1969—in contrast to 1963—the military advantages of an explosion of such small magnitude that it would not be detected are so slight that this is no longer a genuine problem. The dangers of continuing unlimited underground military explosions far exceed those of undetected explosions.[35]

A third and much more intricate problem relates to the determination of whether an underground explosion serves a military objective and, therefore, is prohibited or serves a peaceful objective and, therefore, is permissible. Since internal inspection of the explosive device will not be an acceptable control, the question is whether acceptable alternatives would furnish adequate safeguards. One permitted safeguard arises from the requirement that the weapon state and the non-weapon state furnish in advance to the IAEA a full description of the contemplated explosion—i.e., a scenario. This control measure goes a long way toward assuring that the explosion will not serve a military objective. The scenario the interested states would furnish to the IAEA would have to describe a legitimate peaceful purpose and the contemplated explosion would have to be suitable for achieving that purpose.

Nevertheless, the scenario, no matter how logical it is, cannot furnish a complete assurance that the explosion serves no military purpose. It would be possible, though perhaps difficult, to describe a completely peaceful objective and a contemplated explosion calculated to attain that objective, and at the same time for the weapon state to obtain additional military information, as a fringe benefit, so to speak. However, it is also possible through the process of international observation as described by the United States to reduce to a minimum the danger of such a fringe benefit.

The types of military benefits that might be obtained through such explosions come under three categories:

1. Determining whether a novel explosion device is "Go" or "No go." This is the least probable of the military advantages since in view of factors of both expense and public opinion the nuclear weapon state is unlikely to use a device that has not already been thoroughly tested for a peaceful explosion, particularly one on the territory of a non-weapon state. The possibility of achieving this type of a fringe benefit could be completely eliminated through utilizing a device that had been previously stored with the IAEA under circumstances that would prevent its detonation except by a nuclear power. Such custody, provided there was no international inspection of the device,

apparently could come within the definition of international observation, which the United States has put forward. This, however, would not be "the most efficient or optimal way" to deal with the situation, largely because of high costs and complicated procedures.[36] It would seem that except for one specific situation, the possibilities of using the so-called peaceful explosion to determine whether a novel device is Go or No go are sufficiently remote so that they should not require resorting to the awkward and expensive control of placing the device long in advance of the explosion in storage with the IAEA. The one exception would be if a nuclear-weapon state developed a novel device that gave promise of being more suitable for peaceful explosions than tested devices, and wished to conduct a test to determine both whether it was Go or No go and its characteristics. The amendment to the Test Ban Treaty prohibiting all nuclear explosions except peaceful explosions would probably have to except specifically from the general prohibition such device-testing explosions. It is improbable that the non-nuclear weapon states would agree to such an exception unless consent of the IAEA or some other international body was required in order to conduct the explosion. The IAEA could condition its consent on establishment of adequate controls.

2. A second and more probable military advantage would arise from obtaining detailed measurements of the magnitude and character of the explosion through prompt diagnostics. To obtain such measurements, however, it is necessary to install a vast amount of recording instrumentation including cables visible at the surface above the explosion. Such instrumentation can easily be observed by the IAEA personnel.

3. The third type of military benefit would arise from examination of the radioactive debris after the explosion. No cables or recordings could take the place of an actual "drill back" at the explosion site. However, any such drill back could be detected by the international observers.[37] It is, therefore, suggested that the international observation the United States is recommending give reasonable assurance that military advantages will not be obtained from the underground peaceful explosions.

AMENDING THE LIMITED TEST BAN TREATY TO PERMIT EXPLOSIONS FOR PEACEFUL PURPOSES EVEN THOUGH THE EXPLOSIONS VENT AND TO PROHIBIT ALL OTHER NUCLEAR EXPLOSIONS

In the main, the control problems under this hypothesis are similar to those described where the explosion does not vent. However, some differences must be noted.

First, contrary to the expectations of several years ago, the IAEA will not have to establish a quota of permitted fallout and use this as a factor in determining which explosions shall have the go-ahead signal. Apparently, progress is sufficiently rapid so that by the time "nuclear explosion technology becomes an established industrial tool,"[38] and is available for venting explosions conducted by a weapon state in the territory of a non-weapon state, fallout from the explosive device will be minimal.[39]

Second, if the so-called peaceful explosion were in the atmosphere, the possible military benefits from the explosion would indeed be vast. However, there are no known peaceful applications of nuclear energy that would require explosions in the atmosphere.[40]

Third, the explosions that vent fundamentally may all be described as cratering explosions that take place below the surface, but not so far below as those that do not vent. From the standpoint of obtaining military benefits, there is little difference between these explosions and the non-venting explosions. Of course, all of these explosions will be detected. The possibility of military benefits as in the case of the underground explosions will be limited by the necessity of an advance scenario of the peaceful objective and also by the fact that any military benefits could be realized only through exceedingly complex instrumentation or extensive drill backs after the explosion, both of which would be detected by international observation.

Fourth, a cratering explosion solely to test a new device presents the same problems as an underground explosion for the same purpose. In the absence of reciprocal inspection, the IAEA should be authorized to veto such an explosion.

Fifth, a further protection against military advantages arising from a venting explosion is the simple factor of time. It is becoming increasingly apparent that practical applications for the crater type of peaceful explosions are a number of years away.

Conclusions

Time is a favorable factor in the prognosis for successful international control of Plowshare. If international endeavors such as the SALT talks result in a series of further steps to lessen the possibilities of nuclear proliferation and to set limits on the arms race, it is logical that an international atmosphere will evolve that will make possible more intrusive types of inspection and observation than those presently acceptable to the Soviet Union in its own territory. The presently available controls seem reasonably adequate, both to prevent non-nuclear weapon states from acquiring weapons technology through peaceful explosions, and to furnish fairly good assurance that weapon states will not obtain military benefits from such explosions, if and when the Limited Nuclear Test Ban Treaty is amended to prohibit all military explosions.

In short, *if* continuing progress takes place in the next ten years toward international detente in arms control, a system of international control of peaceful explosions that would give complete assurance against their use to obtain nuclear weapon advantages is a probability. If, on the other hand, we do not have such progress, it seems clear that neither the Non-Proliferation Treaty nor the Limited Test Ban Treaty will survive for as much as fifteen years. The non-weapon states and possibly the weapon states will exercise the rights given them to renounce both treaties. Therefore, in the absence of an improvement in the international atmosphere during the next ten to fifteen years, the whole problem of control of peaceful explosions to prevent nuclear proliferation is likely to become academic.

These conclusions on time limitations in general dovetail with similar conclusions on time limits for other measures to prevent nuclear proliferation such as those required to prevent the spread of uncontrolled fissionable material derived from power reactors throughout the world. The entire panorama emphasizes the extremely short deadline required to work out the international control system necessary to prevent "proliferation unlimited," which in the absence of such a system will be with us in the middle 1980's—perhaps in 1984.

Part 3   Global Security

10

Threat, Reassurance, and Nuclear Proliferation

Joseph I. Coffey

This chapter will consider the kinds of threats that nuclear-armed states may pose to non-nuclear states, the consequent effect upon the impetus to nuclear proliferation, and ways in which the United States can help to assure the security of non-nuclear states and thus reduce any propensities to seek nuclear weapons. It will also look at obstacles to such actions by the United States, whatever their sources or their natures. It will do so in the context of a future world very much like the present one, i.e., a world wherein the United States and the Soviet Union are simultaneously cooperating and competing with one another, and where fears and tensions still persist—albeit, hopefully, at a reduced level.

Types of Threats

In any analysis of these issues, it is necessary to begin by recognizing that nuclear weapons confer enormous advantages upon the country possessing them, and can offset imbalances in population, industrial potential, natural resources, and other components of military power. Even a token nuclear power, with a dozen bombs and embryonic delivery capabilities, could make damaging strikes against selected cities. With slightly larger, but still modest, capabilities, it could neutralize or destroy an opponent's conventional forces, so that if France were still concerned about invasion by Germany, the *force de frappe* should reassure her. And with relatively few nuclear weapons, one state could completely devastate another.[1]

It is obvious that in any conflict between nuclear and non-nuclear states, the latter could find themselves virtually helpless. For instance, the Chinese

Communists could, with fewer than a dozen weapons, not only neutralize or destroy the Nationalist forces on Quemoy (amounting to almost one-third of Chiang Kai-Shek's army), but also knock out the air and naval bases on Taiwan, thus making virtually impossible any Nationalist effort to succor the defenders of Quemoy or to recapture the island. And with just two or three crude nuclear bombs the United Arab Republic could wreak enormous damage on Haifa and Tel Aviv. Even if this were not enough to force an Israeli surrender, it would probably so disrupt the political-economic structure as to give the conventional Arab forces a good chance of success. Hence, those states not possessing nuclear weapons may rightfully be concerned about the consequences of a nuclear strike by present or potential nuclear powers.

In addition, non-nuclear states must also consider the extent to which the mere possession of nuclear weapons by unfriendly powers may constitute a threat. For instance, they may view such weapons as precluding their own use of military force to secure "valid" national objectives. If, in the illustration above, it was the Israelis rather than the Egyptians who possessed nuclear weapons, the latter would certainly regard these as an impediment to any attempt to "liberate" Palestine by embarking on a fourth Arab-Israeli War. Or they may fear that a nuclear-armed opponent might itself initiate conventional attacks, relying on the deterrent effect of its nuclear weapons to preclude or to limit any conventional response by the country invaded. This, indeed, seems to be the concern not only of India with respect to possible Chinese Communist encroachments on its northern border, but also of West Germany with respect to possible Soviet aggression in Europe.

Politically, non-nuclear states may be concerned lest the acquisition of nuclear weapons induce potential opponents to behave more aggressively, to intensify their political and psychological pressures, and to take other actions that could lead to a confrontation between the armed forces of the two countries. They must also consider the likelihood that the possession of nuclear weapons would make these opponents more difficult to deal with, and able to push harder for a favorable resolution of any crisis or confrontation. Further, non-nuclear states may be worried that nuclear-armed states may attempt to practice nuclear blackmail, i.e., to extort political concessions by threatening to use nuclear weapons in the event that these concessions are not granted. And while the successful exploitation of nuclear strength for political advantage may be difficult—if only because the actual use of nuclear weapons carries with it so many potential costs—the threatened countries may not be reassured by this hypothetical complication.

The possibility that non-nuclear states will feel so threatened as to procure nuclear weapons of their own depends not only on the type of threat, but also on its level; i.e., on the capabilities of the nuclear adversary. A state is obviously going to find it difficult to single-handedly build nuclear forces capable of deterring or coping with aggression by one of the superpowers. It may be quicker, cheaper, and easier to form an alliance with the other superpower than to create even a modest deterrent capability. Countries confronting an embryonic nuclear power, however, may be much better able to develop nuclear strike forces capable of inflicting significant damage. Hence they may view the production of nuclear weapons as a feasible and acceptable alternative to politically unpalatable security arrangements. And when a non-nuclear state abuts one that has not yet acquired nuclear weapons, but has the potential to do so, it may at least consider launching disarming strikes against its opponent's nuclear production facilities—a measure that the United States government was urged to take vis-à-vis Communist China. Thus, the choice of responses will depend in large degree upon the level of nuclear armaments held by a potential foe.

It will also depend upon the nature of relations between states. Since Japan may feel less threatened by China than does India, it may have less reason to produce nuclear weapons. And since Italy is allied with one of the two superpowers, it may feel secure even against most threats posed by the other one. This does not mean that alliances in and of themselves suffice for security, or, more importantly, for giving a psychological sense of security since the alliance may be too tenuous, the congruence of interest too transitory, the nuclear power itself may be concerned about counterdeterrence, etc. However, even a thin reed may be better than none, as will be shown below.

Reassuring Measures

If, as suggested previously, non-nuclear states may feel so threatened by present or potential nuclear powers as to consider developing weapons of their own, the United States may wish to reduce the incentive to proliferate by enhancing their sense of security. Although this may be done in a number of ways, ranging from exchanges of visits by heads of state to the provision of military assistance, this paper will concentrate upon four measures that seem most likely to be persuasive: (1) the issuance of unilateral or multilateral security guarantees, either outside of or through the United Nations; (2) the establishment of alliance relationships; (3) the deployment of troops to the country or countries concerned; (4) the dissemination of nuclear weapons; i.e., their distribution to the armed forces of another country under strict and secure American control.

Security Guarantees

From the point of view of a non-nuclear state, the ideal "security guarantee" would probably be a promise by one or more nuclear powers to come to its assistance should it be attacked by, or threatened by, still another nuclear power. To the extent that such a guarantee extended the "nuclear umbrella" over the non-nuclear state, it could both deter a nuclear strike and provide reassurance against nuclear blackmail. To the extent that the promised assistance included support against conventional attacks, it could ease fears of local incursions. And to the extent that the promises were buttressed by staff talks, military aid, and troop deployments to adjacent areas, they could, even in the absence of formal commitments, be made more meaningful to all concerned.

At the moment, the American security guarantee falls considerably short of this mark. The declaration of October, 1964, by President Johnson said only that if non-nuclear states ". . . need our strong support against some threat of nuclear blackmail, then they will have it." Secretary of State Rusk interpreted this statement to mean that a country ". . . specifically threatened with the use of nuclear weapons, would have the entire international community, including the United States, register its support in whatever appropriate way would be necessary in the circumstances."[2] It does not seem likely that the United States would offer stronger guarantees against a nuclear strike, nor commit itself to furnish troops to repel a conventional attack, in part because of reluctance to treat neutrals better than it treats its own allies and in part because of concern lest these measures automatically involve it in any conflict between a nuclear power and a non-nuclear one.

To some extent these risks and commitments may be reduced by joint nuclear guarantees by the United States, the Soviet Union, and (largely for symbolic reasons) the United Kingdom. So far, however, the only joint guarantee is that which these three powers gave in conjunction with the Non-Proliferation Treaty,[3] and this may leave something to be desired. For one thing, it offers guarantees only against nuclear aggression or the threat of such aggression, thereby leaving open the possibility of conventional operations, such as a Soviet thrust into West Germany. For another, it covers only parties to the treaty, leaving exposed countries that have not signed, such as India. For a third, it implies that assistance will be given only if all three nuclear-weapon states that are parties to the treaty join in so doing,[4] and it specifically provides that such assistance will be given through the Security Council, where each of the guarantors (as well as France and Nationalist China) has a veto.[5] And while both the resolution and various declaratory statements make reference to the ". . . inherent right of individual or collective self-defense . . . ." under Article 51 of the United Nations Charter, this is apparently intended as an assurance to present allies rather than as extension of American commitments. In fact, Secretary Rusk testified that the new arrangements would not obligate the United States to take any actions outside of those already required by the UN Charter and by existing treaties of alliance.[6]

Even so, the various assurances given by and in connection with Security Council Resolution 255 might be more meaningful to non-nuclear states if it were not for three other problems. The first is that some states may feel threatened by one of the guarantors; thus, West Germany for a time thought of requiring a specific pledge of nuclear non-aggression from the Soviet Union as a precondition to German adherence to the Non-Proliferation Treaty. Another is that the guaranteeing powers may not always see eye-to-eye on actions to be taken, especially if the alleged threat to use nuclear weapons is made by or directed against one of their allies. And a third is that the already difficult task of acting through the Security Council will become virtually impossible if and when Communist China (against whom Resolution 255 was obviously aimed) secures its "rightful" seat as a permanent member of the Security Council—and with it the prerogative of vetoing any proposed operations. Thus, the prospect that either the unilateral American guarantee of 1964 or the multilateral one of 1968 will markedly assuage the fears and concerns of non-nuclear states seems small indeed.

Alliance Relationships

Another way to warn off and ward off attacks by potential aggressors is through multilateral alliances and bilateral security arrangements. While these may have had the desired effect of inhibiting major assaults on the allies of the United States, they have not precluded the use of force (as in the Chinese Communist operations against Quemoy in 1958) nor the threat of force (as in the Soviet Declaration of 1960 that it would bomb air fields on which American "spy planes" were based). Nor have they fully alleviated concerns lest a nuclear-armed state launch conventional operations under the cover of its own "nuclear umbrella," or undertake "preventive actions," such as an air strike against facilities for separating enriched fissionable materials, which might not provoke an American response. And finally, even those allies who are firmly convinced that the United States will react to overt aggression are not necessarily certain that it will support them in the event of attempts to encroach on their "rights," such as that of access to West Berlin or that of controlling passage through the Dardanelles.

Furthermore, some countries may be unwilling to enter into an alliance with the United States, as India certainly is, or may be unable to induce the United States to give specific and formal guarantees of their territorial integrity, as in the case of Israel. Moreover, it should be noted that the United States, under the so-called Nixon Doctrine, is limiting the ways in which it will uphold its commitments and is seeking to reduce those commitments, in order to bring them more in line both with military capabilities and with political willingness to engage in military operations overseas. Thus, security arrangements in and of themselves may not provide satisfactory assurances to non-nuclear states, even should further alliances be established.

Troop Deployments

To buttress such assurances, the United States has stationed American troops in some areas overseas. In the event of a conventional assault, U.S. forces, such as the armored cavalry regiments along the East German border, could immediately engage the invader. If necessary, nuclear-armed units, such as the battalions of Pershing missiles in NATO Europe, could blunt such an assault by launches against enemy assembly areas, communications centers, depots, etc. And longer-range elements, such as F-104 fighter-bombers or carrier aircraft, could strike at an aggressor's nuclear weapons sites or against targets in his homeland.

Perhaps more important than the military contribution of such forces is their political significance. At the very least, American troops on allied soil are "hostages to fortune," whose presence increases the likelihood of American involvement should any attack occur. Such involvement is even more likely if U.S. forces are stationed at or near probable targets of attack, such as air fields, naval bases, etc., or if they are of a kind (like the fighter-interceptor squadrons in Japan) that may participate in any defensive actions taken. And if the units are nuclear-armed, the possibility of escalation also increases. That such factors are important is evidenced by the unhappiness of the Turks when the American IRBM's were removed following the Cuban Missile Crisis and "replaced" by submarine-launched POLARIS missiles in the Mediterranean Sea.

However, the stationing of American troops in allied countries also creates problems for those countries. It may mean not only the host country's political alignment with the United States, but its possible involvement in conflicts not arising directly out of threats to itself, for which reason Japan has sought to limit the American use of Japanese airfields. Or the presence of U.S. forces may seem provocative to a nuclear-armed neighbor, as the units of the Strategic Air Command based around the periphery of the Soviet Union have seemed to the leaders of that country. Furthermore, the deployment of troops to one friendly country may impair relations with another. Finally, it should be noted that American units may not be welcome, as in the United Arab Republic, or that the United States may be unwilling to dispatch them, as to Israel. Thus, the ability of U.S. forces to convey reassurance to threatened countries may be limited by the perceptions and the policies of those countries, as well as by those of the United States itself.

Dissemination of Nuclear Weapons

Another way in which threatened countries have sought reassurance, and the United States has attempted to give it, is by the dissemination of nuclear weapons and systems for their delivery; thus, Germans pilot nuclear-armed fighter-bombers, Italians man Honest John rockets, etc. Even though the warheads for these weapon systems remain under U.S. control, and no allied soldier can employ them of his own volition, their mere presence enhances the military capabilities of the country concerned, and may well induce caution on the part of a potential aggressor. Dissemination gives evidence of U.S. support, raises the prospect of U.S. involvement, and increases the danger that a local confrontation or conflict may escalate into nuclear war. It may help deter even low-level incursions or encroachments by a nuclear-armed state, since it may partially nullify that state's own nuclear shield, and stiffen the will to resist of the threatened country. In short, dissemination of nuclear weapons (or even of delivery systems for such weapons, like the 155 mm. guns on Quemoy) can both minimize threats to the security of non-nuclear states and enhance their confidence.

This by no means implies that nuclear dissemination is the answer to all prayers. For one thing, some countries might not accept U.S. nuclear weapons at all, and others, even if they decided to do so, might object to the American presence that goes with them. For another, the dissemination of nuclear weapons may be viewed as virtually tantamount to proliferation, and hence may arouse fears and tensions or induce third countries to acquire nuclear weapons of their own. For a third, the warheads and delivery vehicles provided may not match the perceived threat. Thus, some Germans have argued that NATO forces in Europe should have missiles capable of reaching Moscow. And finally, the fact that these nuclear weapons are still under American control may lead to differences over the exact nature of that control, the circumstances under which the weapons might be used, and the question of who decides on their use, and after what consultations.

Limits of Reassurance

In sum, each of the four measures discussed can enhance the sense of security of a threatened country and thereby militate against a decision to produce nuclear weapons. Whether these measures will suffice depends not only on the nature and the imminence of the threat, but on the willingness of the United States to issue specific guarantees, to enter into security arrangements, to dispatch troops to the area and/or to loan nuclear weapons to the armed forces of a potential nth power. It may depend also on the willingness of that nth power to pay the price of reassurance, in terms of association with the United States or the acceptance of an American military presence. Where it is otherwise inclined, or wishes to preserve its freedom of action, reassuring measures may be rejected in favor of the unilateral development of national nuclear forces.

Such a decision may also be reached if reassuring measures are tried and found wanting; i.e., if the UN guarantee does not preclude a nuclear power from blackmailing an opponent, or if support is not forthcoming during a confrontation with that nuclear power. In fact, proliferation is more likely to occur following a crisis the outcome of which is disadvantageous than as the result of a deliberate decision to counter potential threats. For this reason, reassuring measures must be judged as much on their usefulness in managing crises as on their ability to instill a long-term sense of security vis-à-vis nuclear-armed neighbors.

Fortunately, nuclear guarantees, alliance arrangements, and other indications of support may have more impact when war seems imminent, since all concerned will probably view them as committing the United States to resist aggression against the nation so supported. Similarly, the provision of military aid, the dispatch of troops, and the dissemination of nuclear weapons will all have greater meaning if done during a crisis. Moreover, the United States may be more willing to take such actions in response to a specific threat, and the threatened nation may be more inclined to seek U.S. support—as India did in 1962, despite its policy of non-alignment. Thus, all four of the reassuring measures discussed take on new importance in time of crisis or confrontation.

Conversely, they may also be riskier. At the very least, supportive measures carry a greater prospect of American involvement, simply because they represent a U.S. commitment to a not unfavorable crisis outcome. Some measures, such as the stationing of troops in threatened areas, or the provision of advanced weapons requiring technical advisers and maintenance crews, may lead to the deaths of American soldiers and consequent demands for "retaliation," such as those which followed the bombing of the American barracks at Pleiku, in South Vietnam, in 1965. And some types of deployments, such as those of nuclear-armed planes, may seem so provocative that they could exacerbate the crisis rather than ameliorate it. Hence, the United States may be reluctant to take those steps that would have the greatest effect, particularly if the country threatened is not already tied closely to the United States or if the issue at stake is not vital in terms of American interests. There are ways of minimizing these risks, through coordinated action by the United States and the Soviet Union or through joint interposition under United Nations auspices. These, however, may result in measures less favorable to the defending power than steps taken unilaterally by the United States, simply because of the necessity for accepting compromises in order to obtain Soviet agreement or United Nations approval.

U.S. Policy and Nuclear Proliferation

Looked at solely in terms of national security, the impetuses to proliferate may seem very strong and the prospects for meaningful offset measures very weak, since many of the latter may be unacceptable, unlikely of implementation, or of marginal impact. In order, however, to judge the possibility of success—and therefore the demands placed upon U.S. policy—one must look in perspective at the threats to various countries and at measures that may reassure them concerning those threats.

The first possibility is that potential nuclear powers such as Japan, Italy, Sweden, Switzerland, and West Germany may feel so threatened by the Soviet Union as to consider developing nuclear weapons unless their security is otherwise guaranteed.[7] At the moment, however, the threat of Soviet aggression seems too remote to stimulate Japanese nuclear weapons development, especially since the Japanese are well aware of their inability to compete with the Soviet Union in building strategic strike forces and are seemingly satisfied with the protection afforded by their treaty of alliance with the United States. The same may be true of Italy, which, moreover, has the further assurances provided by participation in the planning of NATO nuclear strategy and by the presence of U.S. nuclear weapons on Italian soil.

Sweden and Switzerland are safeguarded to some extent by their geographic isolation and by their traditional neutrality; moreover, there is little or no evidence that these two countries feel threatened by the Soviet Union. Unless there is a significant upsurge in Soviet bellicosity, therefore, it is unlikely that the United States will have to consider additional measures designed to reassure or support these countries.

The same cannot be said with respect to West Germany, which apparently still feels threatened by the Soviet Union despite the assurances provided by membership in NATO, by the presence of large numbers of American and other allied forces, by the dissemination of nuclear weapons, and by specific and repeated American commitments. While it is possible that German fears might be assuaged by the creation of multinational or multilateral nuclear forces, embodying a German contingent of one type or another, attempts to organize such a force have so far failed. Moreover, it is unlikely that any conceivable organization could meet the conflicting requirements of West Germany and its NATO allies—including the United States. Fortunately, other measures, such as participation in the NATO Nuclear Planning Group, may partially satisfy German aspirations; changes in the implementation (if not in the basic concept) of NATO strategy may bolster German confidence in the deterrent; mutual and balanced reductions in forces in Central Europe may alleviate German concerns; and alterations in Soviet policy may affect German perceptions of the threat to its security.[8] Since formidable technical, military, and political obstacles to the German development of a meaningful nuclear deterrent remain, one may hope that future German governments will continue the policy of past ones, and eschew the acquisition of nuclear weapons.

A second possibility is that countries such as Australia, Japan, and India may become so worried about the behavior of a nuclear-armed China as to develop weapons of their own. While there have been some indications of such worry on the part of Australia, its remoteness, the low likelihood of any confrontation with Communist China, and the protection afforded by the ANZUS treaty should all alleviate concern. Should they not do so, the United States could—and might have to—make available nuclear warheads (under U.S. control), deploy American troops to the area, or install there nuclear-armed defensive missiles, under joint command. In brief, a number of American actions could alleviate possible Australian concerns without being so difficult, or so provocative, as to pose problems for U.S. policy-makers.

The situation vis-à-vis Japan is very different, in that the Japanese would probably be much less willing to introduce additional U.S. troops, to allow these to bring with them nuclear weapons, or even to accept U.S.-controlled warheads for their own or for jointly manned weapons systems. While the same factors that militate against such measures—notably, the antipathy to nuclear weapons resulting from the bombing of Hiroshima and Nagasaki—also weigh heavily against domestic nuclear development, the latter may be viewed as more likely to preserve Japanese independence of action, as well as to enhance Japanese prestige and influence and to spur technical progress. Fortunately, the Japanese do not seem to feel threatened by Communist China (or by the Soviet Union), but if this feeling should change (or if they should conclude, as some among the military apparently have, that their overall interests can be secured only by nuclear weapons), they may be more inclined to build their own nuclear deterrent than to rely solely upon the protection afforded by the American one. Hence, the United States may have to rely more on political and psychological actions to assuage latent Japanese fears than upon military measures. And it may, if it is seriously interested in precluding Japanese nuclear proliferation, have to alter its views about the role Japan should play in the Far East, and seek to limit Japanese military commitments and defense forces, rather than to expand them.

India may present even more of a problem, as it does fear Chinese

Communist aggression, is non-aligned, and has repeatedly criticized as inadequate the guarantees offered by the nuclear powers. While it might, in a future crisis, again accept American assistance, it would undoubtedly seek similar aid from the Soviet Union and the United Kingdom, and might well insist that any deployments of troops, basing of weapons, etc., be carried out jointly by all the nuclear guarantors—and under Indian control. If the threat increased slowly, rather than emerging suddenly, India would probably ask the nuclear powers for firm, joint guarantees; failing these, it would almost certainly build nuclear weapons of its own. Thus, reassurances to India might well require not only an extension of U.S. commitments, but also the formulation of complex politico-military arrangements for making good on these commitments—with the consequent necessity of justifying these arrangements both to the American public and to the world at large.

A third set of problems could arise in the case of countries concerned lest a hostile neighbor "go nuclear." One example is that of Israel, which may fear that the Soviet Union would give or disseminate nuclear weapons to the United Arab Republic. Another example is the United Arab Republic itself, which may be worried about the Israeli development of a token nuclear force. A third is Pakistan, which may well become alarmed should India attempt to acquire a nuclear capability, in which case the Pakistanis might look abroad (i.e., to Communist China) for nuclear weapons of their own. And finally, it is conceivable that if Argentina develops nuclear weapons (as was hinted at a recent Pugwash Conference[9]) Brazil may also do so, although more for political reasons than because Argentina would pose a military threat.

Even in these few, specialized cases, the United States will face great difficulties in reducing incentives to proliferate. In most of these countries American ability to influence defense policy is limited, and its willingness to take more stringent measures (such as abrogating economic assistance, controlling the flow of funds, imposing trade embargoes, etc.) is tempered by recognition that these may be counterproductive. Furthermore, the United States is reluctant to give hard and fast security guarantees to non-nuclear nations, especially at the expense of further antagonizing countries such as the United Arab Republic and India, which may consider themselves threatened by American support of Israel or of Pakistan. It is even more reluctant to deploy troops to new areas, to disseminate nuclear weapons to additional countries, or to loosen the controls it exercises over those weapons. Moreover, it is (and should be) concerned lest unilateral actions, however desirable they may seem to a threatened country, again embroil the United States in a confrontation with the Soviet Union, which may be supporting the other side.

Considerations such as those outlined above suggest that it will be difficult to formulate a policy designed to persuade potential nuclear powers that they need not acquire nuclear weapons in order to safeguard their national interests. Certainly the United States cannot succeed simply by reminding probable nth powers that their forces may be small, vulnerable, provocative, etc. Such an effort not only failed in the case of France, but is not necessarily correct in terms of the kinds of threats that many of these powers may face. Nor can the United States argue that the present nuclear guarantees will suffice, since these contain too many ambiguities and gaps to provide assurance under all circumstances against the use of nuclear weapons or the threat to use them.

Thus, the first step in the difficult process of policy formulation should be to study intensively the kinds of threats that may induce non-nuclear powers to acquire nuclear weapons. To the extent that these threats seem invalid, efforts might be made to induce the country concerned to re-examine them. (By way of illustration, no one to date has indicated how "nuclear blackmail" can really be carried out if the blackmailing state is unwilling to accept the risk of actually using nuclear weapons.) To the extent that they seem valid (or are so strongly held that they become "real," which is the same thing), the United States should try to ascertain which American responses may be reassuring, the conditions under which these can and should be made, how to avoid being unduly provocative, etc.

In this connection, a number of possibilities seem worth examining. Among them are specific warnings to a potential aggressor and specific assurances of support in the event of such aggression; the provision of defensive armaments (such as surface-to-air missiles); and the deployment to the threatened country of American forces similarly equipped to defend against air or missile strikes. More provocative, but still worth looking at, are the redeployment to that country, or to areas nearby, of tactical nuclear forces (such as carrier-borne aircraft or fighter squadrons) or even of strategic bombers, which can serve as visible symbols of support. And not to be ruled out is the dissemination of nuclear weapons—hopefully on a limited, temporary, and strictly controlled basis.

Once it has decided what measures would be most meaningful, the United States might consider how to carry them out. In view of the probable unacceptability to many countries of unilateral American support, the United States might place special emphasis upon multilateral actions, as envisioned under Resolution 255 of the UN Security Council. In view of the possible difficulty of obtaining the approval of the Security Council (especially if Communist China is a member), the United States might also devise other ways of obtaining UN endorsement, as through an updated "Uniting for Peace" resolution, or through the establishment of a "Special Committee" of nuclear weapon states to implement the UN guarantee. And because of the difficulties and dangers of going against the wishes of the Soviet Union, the United States might want to seek Soviet assent to unilateral American actions and Soviet cooperation in any multiparty ones. Furthermore, U.S.-Soviet collaboration in devising and presenting for consideration measures to safeguard non-nuclear powers from threats by nuclear-armed states could in itself reduce the fear of such threats and minimize the need for additional (and unpalatable) extensions of American commitments and guarantees, and for the involvement of American forces.

As noted earlier, joint measures, or measures taken under United Nations auspices, would probably be less likely to insure a favorable crisis outcome than those which the United States might take unilaterally. They would, however, also be considerably less risky. Moreover, it does not necessarily hold that the United States itself would in every instance be willing to take sides; in a conflict between the United Arab Republic and nuclear-armed Israel, or between Pakistan and a potentially nuclear India, the United States might favor a policy of interposition rather than one of intervention. Even relatively small forces deployed between, say, Israeli and Egyptian armies are likely to have a considerable effect, and may be much more successful in dampening a crisis or in precluding nuclear war than larger deployments in favor of one side or another. This would be particularly true if the forces interposed were defensive rather than offensive, and were multinational, rather than all-American. And while these requirements may give rise to military or technical difficulties, they are clearly in line with the concepts and the proposed procedures of the Non-Proliferation Treaty.

Implications for the Future

If the United States should, in fact, adopt policies designed to reduce the incentives to proliferation (and the military advantages of so doing) this would have a number of implications. For one thing, it would probably require that the United States try to settle disputes that could lead to nuclear proliferation (as in some instances it has been attempting to do) rather than let the dispute drag on. For another, it might require the United States to dampen conflicts in a more or less impartial manner, rather than to buttress one party against the other. For a third, it would certainly require the United States to cooperate closely with the Soviet Union, whose collaboration would be essential in coping with some threats and helpful in dealing with others. And this, in turn, would necessitate an understanding by both countries of the limits of permissible action in today's world. None of these will be easy, and some of them could be difficult to justify to both domestic and foreign publics.

A policy aimed at precluding further nuclear proliferation could also affect the composition of present and programmed American forces. If at all possible, these should include mobile units for air and missile defense, armed with conventional rather than with nuclear warheads, which could make difficult the delivery of nuclear weapons by technologically less advanced countries. (This may, for example, suggest the re-equipping of two or three aircraft carriers so that they are more effective for air defense purposes, even at the expense of cutting down on their strike capabilities.) If the threat warrants it—and if any arms control agreement authorizes it—they might also include more sophisticated strategic defense, such as seaborne antiballistic missile systems, even where these require the use of nuclear warheads. (In that case, however, the United States would also have to adopt special safeguards with respect to the construction, control, and utilization of such weapons, in order to insure that they were neither provocative nor escalatory.) And since American troops might well find themselves operating in conjunction not only with allied units, but also with those from countries that are now neutral, or even hostile, U.S. forces should be prepared to overcome problems arising from different weapons system designs, employment doctrines, communications procedures, etc.

All this is not to suggest that reassuring or supportive measures necessitate larger American forces; instead, the kinds of actions suggested above could be implemented by a change in emphasis within current (or smaller) military programs. Nor is it to argue that nuclear proliferation can be inhibited only by policies calling for greater U.S. involvement and more forceful U.S. actions vis-à-vis potential aggressors; as we have seen in the case of West Germany, measures to ameliorate actual or perceived threats may offer more promise than measures to cope with such threats. Furthermore, it may well be that American perceptions of future threats and of programs required to deal with them have fed the fears of potential nuclear powers. (After all, if Communist China's development of a few ICBM's required the United States, despite its overwhelming strategic nuclear power, to install ballistic missile defenses, why shouldn't Australia worry?) Until the United States comes to assess more accurately the threats to its own security it is unlikely to persuade others to reassess the threats to theirs, and unless the United States itself is prepared to safeguard its security by means other than armaments build-ups, it is unlikely to induce others to renounce forever the acquisition or development of nuclear weapons. Thus, in a larger sense, success in precluding further nuclear proliferation may depend both on a change in American views of the world and on alterations in American policy designed to bring about more peaceful and cooperative relations among the nations of that world.

11 Renunciation of Nuclear Weapons Use

Richard A. Falk

A persistent, if muted, theme in discussions of arms control and disarmament questions has been concerned with the status of nuclear weapons. The renunciation of the option to use nuclear weapons can be made either in the form of a unilateral declaration of official policy or as an essential ingredient of an international convention. The Soviet Union and China have already made unilateral declarations of policy,[1] and the Soviet Union, despite its conflict with China, has proposed as recently as 1967 an international convention that embodies an absolute prohibition on initiating uses of nuclear weapons.[2]

Note that the renunciation of the nuclear option refers only to *initiating use.* A government retains possession of nuclear weapons, control over research and development of further weapons technology, and control over deployment. Most important of all, a government retains a residual option to retaliate with nuclear weapons against a prior use of nuclear weapons. This prior use may be a violation by another state of its own renunciation of its option to use nuclear weapons, or it could arise in the event it has never made such a renunciation. The renunciation of the nuclear option may be conditioned on reciprocity, but there is no reason why this should be so, and it has not been so conditioned in the Soviet and Chinese instances.

A renunciation of the nuclear option is not limited by time, place, or context. In this sense it is a *categorical* norm. At the same time this general

The author wishes to acknowledge the assistance of Claudia Cords in the preparation of this manuscript. As well, I was much benefited by conversation with and comments from Harold Feiveson of Princeton's Center of International Studies.

renunciation can be associated with limited renunciations, such as are embodied in ideas of nuclear-free zones,[3] or in restrictions placed upon the nuclear option, such as a commitment to use nuclear weapons only on national territory or only against targets outside populated areas.

There are some reasons to favor making the *categorical* rule more *absolute* by denying the right of reprisal, research and development, and even possession, but such steps remain too far removed from political attitudes to stand any chance of even receiving serious appraisal. Hence, attention here will be limited to a renunciation of the nuclear option, namely, of the claimed right to initiate the use of nuclear weapons.

A great majority of the non-nuclear powers, as well as the Soviet Union and China, have advocated prohibitions on the use of nuclear weapons. The General Assembly in 1961, over the vigorous, if somewhat quiet, opposition of the U.S. government, passed by a vote of 55-20-26 Resolution 1653 (XVI), which declared that the use of nuclear weapons would violate the letter and spirit of the United Nations Charter and constitute a crime against mankind.[4] Subsequent resolutions of the General Assembly have, by more one-sided votes, called upon governments to conclude an agreement prohibiting the use of nuclear weapons and have invoked General Assembly Resolution 1653, with approval, as authority.[5] The U.S. government has continued to oppose all formal and international efforts to withdraw legitimacy from nuclear weapons. It seems appropriate to examine carefully the grounds of this opposition both in response to the apparent sentiments of world public opinion and in view of the terrible consequences of recourse to nuclear weapons.[6]

Legal Status of Nuclear Weapons

The present legal status of nuclear weapons remains in considerable doubt. The UN has made it clear that more than two thirds of its voting membership regard the initiating use of nuclear weapons as both illegal and criminal. On the other hand, most specialists continue to deny that the General Assembly possesses a law-creating capacity in relation to a determined minority of dissenting sovereign states.[7] The United States and the NATO group seem to be an important enough dissenting minority with respect to the status of nuclear weapons to block the creation of a new rule of prohibition by the UN either through majority vote or a declaratory statement as to the character of pre-existing law. The General Assembly can merely *declare* the status of nuclear weapons and provide guidance as to the proper interpretation of this status by the government. As yet, however, there is no strong sense of obligation on the part of dissenting governments to accord respect to resolutions they have voted against, even if their dissenting vote is not supported by enough other states to block formal passage in accordance with UN voting rules.

It is possible to argue, however, that the use of nuclear weapons, at least against populated areas, would be illegal under prior valid prohibitions upon weapons and tactics of indiscriminate destruction and lethal poison. Some international law experts have argued to this effect; however, others have disagreed, contending that nuclear weapons are a new development, not covered by earlier rules, and that the legality of their use depends on particular circumstances.[8] There is thus no clear consensus of experts about the status of these weapons.

Additional considerations serve to underline the basic condition of ambiguity. The United States has refrained from using or overtly threatening to use nuclear weapons during either the Korean War or the Vietnam War. Such conduct suggests the emergence of a subtle tradition of non-use, at least under circumstances of limited war for limited ends. On the other hand, the official U.S. position insists on the right to initiate a nuclear response to what it regards as enemy aggression. Official service manuals conclude that nuclear weapons cannot be considered as prohibited weapons of war in the absence of an explicit rule.[9]

The ambiguity in the legal status of nuclear weapons is reinforced by persistent international efforts to achieve an explicit rule of prohibition either in the form of a series of declarations by nuclear powers or by a binding treaty rule of prohibition. Such efforts would be largely superfluous if the legal status of these weapons were already clear to principal governments. Furthermore, the United States and the NATO group base a major portion of their military planning upon their right and willingness to initiate a nuclear response to certain forms of non-nuclear provocation. Hence, it is impossible to infer any *de facto* prohibition upon a first use of nuclear weapons, and the desirability of some move in that direction remains an important and controversial arms control issue.

The approach of this chapter is directed by two guidelines:

1. A judgment that the issue of legal status is not presently resolved by UN action, attitudes of governments, or commentary by experts in international law.

2. A judgment that the United States opposition to a rule of prohibition continues to be the critical obstacle to its emergence.

In light of these two assessments I propose to center inquiry on the arguments used to support the American position and the counterarguments. In the concluding section, I advance a brief argument for changing the American position to one of support for either a declaratory statement or a treaty rule that prohibits *an initiating, or first, use* of nuclear weapons.

Grounds of U.S. Opposition

In various official and semiofficial settings the United States government has made clear its refusal to agree to any general ban on use of nuclear weapons. It is important to evaluate the cogency of this refusal, but first we need to understand its basis.

European Security

For a long time the principal reason that the United States, together with its NATO allies, has claimed the right to initiate the use of nuclear weapons has been to deter a possible Soviet attack upon Western Europe. According to this position, conventional means of defense could not withstand a large-scale Soviet conventional attack and, therefore, Soviet pressure on Western Europe could only be resisted through reliance upon a threat of nuclear response. And, in fact, recent reports on NATO planning have disclosed decisions to deploy nuclear weapons near possible battle frontiers, so as to make clear that even a border-crossing probe by Soviet or Soviet-supported forces in Europe would almost inevitably provoke a nuclear response.[10]

The argument for reliance on nuclear weapons rests on several propositions: (1) the Soviet Union would use military force to conquer, or at least intimidate, Western Europe if it were not deterred from doing so by the prospect of a nuclear response; (2) Western Europe could not, or at any rate would not, develop a deterrent posture adequate to forswear reliance on nuclear weapons; (3) the United States is more concerned with the adequacy of European security than it is with any lessening of world tensions that might result from prohibiting the use of nuclear weapons; (4) the effect of such a prohibition would be to stimulate the development of a credible European *nuclear* deterrent rather than to remove nuclear weapons from a central role in defense planning. Thus, the prohibition would stimulate the proliferation of nuclear weapons—for instance, to West Germany—and would hence have an effect opposite to its intention. There would be no reduction in the reliance upon nuclear weapons, but only a shift away from American control over the decision to initiate the use of nuclear weapons.

Overall World Role

America's far-flung security commitments could only be realistically met, this argument proceeds, if "the nuclear option" is kept open. Such a position rests on a combination of military and political considerations. It has been clearly expressed by the strategist Bernard Brodie: "It is therefore quite possible that we could fight another war in the Far East as large as the Korean War, or even a repetition of that war, without using nuclear weapons—assuming the American people permitted the government to engage again in such a war

.... But surely it would be going about the job the *hard* way, especially since timely indication of readiness to use nuclear weapons is *bound* to have an enormous, and very likely a guaranteed deterrent power." Brodie adds that "[f]ailure to use them under such circumstances would probably have repercussions for the future that would in the net be not to our liking."[11]

Despite the failure to use or even to threaten use of nuclear weapons throughout the Vietnam War, it seems correct to suppose that American military planners value the nuclear option as a residual possibility, to be exercised in non-European theaters of action only in exceptional circumstances. In essence, then, there seems to be a rather important belief that American superiority in nuclear weapons may be useful as a deterrent and as a response in unforeseen circumstances. Such a belief seems to be associated, in official American thinking, with "the stability" of relations between nuclear powers.

In opposition to the Soviet proposal for a treaty prohibition of the use of nuclear weapons, Adrian Fisher, then the U.S. representative in the First Committee of the General Assembly, said that "we must consider the role that the present nuclear forces play in the relatively stable strategic balance which now exists between the major nuclear powers in the world and the effect on that balance of an obligation not to use nuclear weapons under any circumstances." More to the point, Mr. Fisher argued that "the most effective way of minimizing the risk of nuclear war will be through the maintenance of mutual deterrence" and that "[a]s long as such a posture continues, an agreement not to use nuclear weapons, even in self-defense or in retaliation, would be, at worst deceptive—and therefore dangerous—and, at best, unrealistic."[12] Underlying this position is the idea that world peace rests on deterrence and that deterrence extends beyond a nuclear surprise attack to include "aggression" by the adversary.[13]

The Proper Sequence

The United States also contends that a prohibition on the use of nuclear weapons as a first-step measure "puts the cart before the horse, so to speak, or the plough in front of the ox." Mr. Fisher has explained that the "non-use proposal would not be a meaningful document unless something were also done about nuclear stockpiles" and that "the elimination of nuclear weapons from national arsenals could only be accomplished in the context of general and complete disarmament under effective international control."[14] In this view, the nuclear option needs to be maintained as a deterrent to major aggression until the virtual completion of the disarmament process.

Underneath this contention is the belief that the existence of nuclear weapons has maintained the peace during a period of tension and conflict in international history.[15] After World War II, culminating in John Foster Dulles' formulation of a doctrine of "massive retaliation,"[16] the United States rested its security almost completely on its willingness and ability to use nuclear weapons if sufficiently provoked by Communist action. Brodie writes, "Even as late as the Quemoy crisis of 1958, few of our aircraft had bomb-racks suitable for carrying 'conventional' or non-nuclear bombs."[17] More recently, in connection with the *Pueblo* incident, the United States appeared to lack the capacity for an effective non-nuclear assertion of its military power. Reasons of fiscal economy have combined with a sense of technological advantage to stress the role of nuclear weapons in American military planning.

Under such circumstances, any step to curtail the use of nuclear weapons would appear to hurt the United States more than the Soviet Union, especially given the far-flung commitments the United States now has. As such, a prohibition on nuclear weapon use as a first-step measure could be viewed as inconsistent with the sixth principle of the McCloy-Zorin "Joint Statement of Agreed Principles for Disarmament Negotiations" of 1961 that "All measures of general and complete disarmament should be balanced so that at no stage of the implementation of the treaty could any State or group of States gain military advantage and that security is ensured equally for all."[18] Thomas B. Larson writes that "the U.S.S.R. has always favored measures to 'blacken' nuclear weapons."[19] Such a curious contention takes it for granted that Soviet initiatives with regard to prohibition are prompted by a desire to gain one-sided military advantages from making nuclear weapons illegitimate instruments of foreign policy.

A more moderate variant of this position is to view the issue of prohibition as one of bargaining significance. Namely, the United States should receive something from the Soviet Union and possibly China, in exchange for renouncing its right to initiate nuclear response. The exchange has not ever been spelled out by an American official, but it could involve political assurances as to objectives and zonal limitations on troop deployment. This view that a fair bargain should be struck arises from the belief that the United States would be giving up more than other governments by agreeing to the prohibition and that the issue is a suitable one for normal bargaining characteristic of international diplomacy.

Historical Relationship to Nuclear Weapons

The use of atomic weapons in 1945 by the United States against Hiroshima and Nagasaki has a subtle influence on the American attitude toward prohibition proposals. The United States has a defensive attitude toward the legitimacy of these weapons because it has actually made a highly controversial use of nuclear weapons against heavily populated areas and because it is the only country ever to have used these weapons. For instance, a Japanese district court in the *Shimoda* case decided, with the help of three separate expert opinions, that these attacks violated international law because of their highly destructive and indiscriminate character.[20] The U.S. government continues to defend its recourse to atomic weapons, and in part does so by arguing that such weapons are legitimate weapons of war in the absence of a treaty prohibition.

In contrast, the Soviet Union harps on American use of atomic weapons as indicative of an unwillingness to limit the destructive capabilities at the disposal of the United States. The Soviet representative in the First Committee of the UN General Assembly, Lev Mendelevich, accounts for the U.S. attitude by the observation that "the history of nuclear weapons started with the use of those weapons by the United States at Hiroshima and Nagasaki. That is probably what created a sort of complex about the use of nuclear weapons which prevents the United States from adopting a more constructive attitude towards proposals to prohibit the use of nuclear weapons."[21] There does seem to be American resistance to a view of nuclear weapons that would cast a shadow across prior U.S. acts. Such a shadow is, however, already cast by the *Shimoda* decision, by General Assembly Resolution 1653 (XVI), and by world public opinion.

Nature of the Obligation

The United States has been traditionally reluctant to make broad sweeping commitments that might restrict choice in future international situations. In this respect, a prohibition on the use of nuclear weapons might have unfortunate applications that cannot be taken into account in the statement of general principle. The United States tends to favor a *contextual* approach to obligations of this sort, leaving officials free to adapt general rules to specific situations. American opposition to Soviet proposals for an agreed definition of aggression is the most obvious other example of this distrust of general principle.

In addition, a prohibition of this sort can be taken more or less seriously by governments. The United States tends to view itself as more scrupulous than the Soviet Union in honoring an obligation formally undertaken, and therefore as more likely to be subject to a greater restriction of its freedom of action despite the formal equality of the burden. Private comment also emphasizes the greater capacity of a centralized and coercive society, such as the Soviet Union, to maintain nuclear weapons research facilities at a high state of efficiency in the event that nuclear weapons were shifted to the prohibited category than would be possible in the United States.

Finally, there are a variety of uncertainties, perhaps irreducible, that are relied upon to argue against a sweeping prohibition. First of all is the difficulty inherent in offering any precise description of "use" as applicable to nuclear weapons: are threats included? are deployment patterns included? are retaliatory uses confined in scope and scale to initiating uses? Secondly, there are difficulties inherent in the process of implementation: does a government have to act as well as give its formal assent? what happens to the rule of prohibition in the event of non-participation by some nuclear powers? These questions have been raised in a variety of ways in the course of formal debates on the status of nuclear weapons.

The Case Against the U.S. Position

In this section the main refutations of the American arguments will be combined with positive grounds for favoring a categorical form of nuclear weapons prohibition.

U.S. Security Commitments: Europe and Elsewhere

Security interests are diverse for a variety of countries. A precedent set supports comparable claims in a variety of settings. The claim of Europe to defend itself with nuclear weapons against a non-nuclear attack seems like a far-reaching and generally undesirable precedent. Other states confronting serious challenges such as Israel or South Africa would be encouraged to assert a comparable claim. In contrast, the establishment of a global prohibition on the use of nuclear weapons, comparable to the prohibition applicable to poison gas, would tend to discourage reliance on weapons of mass destruction by making such a claim, even in defense, illegitimate.

Security interests extend and vary over time and space. To premise a nuclear option upon a special set of circumstances prevailing at one time in Europe is not consistent with overall interests in avoiding the introduction of nuclear weapons into armed conflict. Besides, in my judgment, no substantial threat of a Soviet attack on Western Europe exists, nor is one likely to exist in the foreseeable future. European capabilities exist to meet Soviet probes and pressures without any reliance on a nuclear option; in fact, the renunciation of nuclear weapons as legitimate instruments of defense may lead to an overall reduction of European tensions and to greater East-West cooperation. In any event, the alleged danger of a massive attack by Soviet conventional armies does not seem to be either credible or significant enough to warrant a system-wide endorsement of the legitimacy of national defense policies based on the nuclear option.

Other American security interests, aside from those associated with the defense of homeland or with participation in UN operations, can be met without reliance on the nuclear option. These security interests, in light of the Vietnam experience, are of doubtful validity, and their elimination might better serve the national interest than would their pursuit. But leaving aside this issue of policy, there seems to be no credible danger to major American interests in any part of the world that could not be dealt with at subnuclear levels of military violence.

Stability and Peace

World stability would be helped, not hindered, by the denuclearization of international relations. All states would be restored to a kind of prenuclear parity that is consistent with the overall objectives of non-proliferation. The nuclear powers, by forswearing the nuclear option, would help to eliminate the distinction between nuclear and non-nuclear powers and would thereby remove one main incentive for the acquisition of nuclear weapons. As the Deputy Foreign Minister of the Soviet Union, Vasily Kuznetsov, expressed the point in a UN debate on the Soviet proposal for a treaty prohibition, ". . . if States undertook not to use nuclear weapons, this would decrease the threat of a nuclear war and would bring us closer to the possibilities of destroying nuclear weapons. The prohibition of the use of nuclear weapons would paralyze this weapon politically."[22] Even if there is no way to establish numerically the impact of a prohibition on the likelihood of nuclear war, there is some reason to believe that the prospects of use would diminish with the establishment of a prohibition. Certainly this correlation underlies all efforts of law to prohibit behavior or instruments of conflict.

The present retention of discretion with respect to the use of nuclear weapons is also not persuasively explained as a way to deter aggression. For one thing, the perception of what constitutes aggression is very subjective and tends to be heavily biased in light of perspective and interests.[23] Governments typically reach contradictory determinations as to the identity of the aggressor in a particular war. Because of this tendency to reach biased judgments, it seems desirable not to entrust national governments with wide responsibilities to define and punish aggression. And especially, given the awesome consequences of nuclear warfare, it seems desirable to limit as clearly and fully as possible the discretion of a government to use these weapons.

The renunciation of the nuclear option would eliminate the temptation to develop doctrines of limited strategic use for nuclear weapons. These doctrines erode the underlying stability of deterrence by their tendency to normalize recourse to nuclear weapons as an instrument of warfare and diplomacy.

In an even more central way, a commitment not to resort to the first use of nuclear weapons would facilitate negotiations on major arms control agreements. The present nuclear posture, based on *extended* deterrence rather than on *minimum* deterrence (i.e., of a nuclear strike), requires ambiguity as to intentions, which expands requirements for nuclear capabilities. The retention of a nuclear option for a variety of contingencies other than retaliation against a nuclear strike makes it very difficult to impose effective restraints on the acquisition of new weapons systems or to impose ceilings on stockpiles. The outcome has been a continuous and expensive peacetime arms race and the accumulation of a huge "overkill" capability. It is only overkill in relation to a certain fixed mission. The weapons are all needed if each plausible mission and theater of use is to be adequately supplied in the event that a contingency arises. Such contingency planning is what extended deterrence is all about.[24]

A Beneficial First Step

To renounce the right to use nuclear weapons first would seem to have a variety of beneficial side effects. First of all, the nature of such a commitment would represent a dramatic effort to return the nuclear genie to its bottle and to defy apostles of technological inevitability. This gesture would also serve to educate and inform people as to the reasons why the nuclear option is dangerous and otherwise undesirable, for instance by its tendency toward inflicting indiscriminate harm.

Secondly, such an act of renunciation would probably, although not assuredly, lead to a slowing of the arms race, including inhibiting to some extent the deployment of ABM and MIRV weapons systems. The focus of nuclear strategy would tend to become unambiguously confined to problems of nuclear reprisal in response to a nuclear surprise attack. There is no question that governments would retain the nuclear reprisal option in the event that the prohibition upon first use came into effect.

Thirdly, the devaluation of the role of nuclear weapons would seem to encourage the substantial reduction of existing stockpiles, thereby further helping the cause of non-proliferation and of general disarmament. A small, highly dispersed, highly mobile second-strike capability would be all that was needed to assure a capacity for nuclear reprisal. Such a capability could be achieved at a fraction of present costs, risks, and energies.

Fourthly, a renunciation of nuclear weapons would tend to satisfy the repeated demands by non-nuclear states for "reciprocity" in arms control negotiations. As such, it could be expected to improve the overall atmosphere for reaching arms control agreements.

The tides of technological fortune change and it is not to be assumed that the United States or any country will necessarily ever want to make use of the nuclear option. It seems desirable to lessen the probability that any government will *initiate* nuclear war *for any reason*. The decision to use atomic weapons against Japanese cities at a time when the war was substantially won by the Allied side further suggests the ease with which a government in the future might vindicate its decision to resort to nuclear weapons.

The renunciation of the nuclear option would help move the United States out beyond the shadow of Hiroshima and Nagasaki. Those atomic attacks, viewed as illegal by the only court that ever examined the question, have influenced the whole turn of the post-World War II world. A prohibition would look toward the future with a real determination to avoid a repetition of nuclear destruction.

The simple undertaking to renounce the nuclear option is a self-enforcing and unambiguous undertaking. It requires no elaborate bargaining, whether put in the form of a series of parallel national declarations of intent or of an international convention.

Norms of prohibition have been proposed and developed for many weapons in the course of international history. As recently as November 25, 1969, President Nixon indicated his support for norms of prohibition applicable to chemical and biological weapons. He also recommended that the United States ratify the 1925 Geneva Protocol prohibiting the use in warfare of poison gases and bacteriological weapons. Mr. Nixon's statement indicated a willingness by the United States to limit its research effort on biological weapons to defensive measures designed to moderate the effects of their use by others, and it solicited recommendations from the Department of Defense as to the proper way to destroy existing stockpiles of bacteriological weapons. The point here is that a norm of prohibition—even without negotiation and enforcement—has been set "as an initiative toward peace." President Nixon's statement went on to say that "by the examples we set today, we hope to contribute to an atmosphere of peace and understanding between nations and among men."[25]

The existence of a nuclear shield undoubtedly helped build a political basis for this action. Nevertheless, the same reasoning used to explain norms of renunciation in the bacteriological and chemical fields is applicable, and with far greater force, to nuclear weapons.

Finally, the formulation of this obligation in *categorical* rather than *contextual* form assures that a certain clarity of standards is achieved. To allow national officials a limited option based on claims that an initiating use of nuclear weapons is for *defensive* purposes or only against *military targets* or under circumstances of *necessity* would reinforce traditions of self-serving discretion that have already hampered every effort to bring law to bear on governments in the area of war and peace. Even a categorical prohibition on first use, which is largely self-defining in content, is vulnerable, of course, to violations. All rules of restraint seek to deter marginal violations by adding respect for enacted law as a consideration in decision-making and planning contexts. In relation to nuclear weapons, there already exists a weak tradition of non-use, principally created by the failure of the United States to use these weapons in Korea and Vietnam, and a rule of prohibition or a declaration of self-denial would merely serve to strengthen such a tradition.

There are also important domestic reasons associated with constitutional democracy that support a renunciation of the nuclear option. The initial use of nuclear weapons would almost always, because of the element of surprise, involve a Presidential decision without benefit of Congressional advice or authorization. A decision to respond with nuclear weapons after their prior use could be undertaken on the basis of broader participation by top officials, which would more closely fulfill expectations about "checks and balances" as an integral element in our form of constitutional democracy.[26]

On Balance

Many difficult questions would arise if serious consideration were to be given by the United States government to a shift of its position on the status of nuclear weapons. Would the United States be unable to uphold its vital interests in a less nuclear world? Suppose nuclear weapons had not been developed, would the political map of the world look significantly different? Of course, we cannot provide real answers to such questions. The assessment of comparative risk is largely based on a series of intuitive judgments that can never be conclusively assessed by measurement or by experience. We cannot know what would have happened had our judgments and policies in the past been different than they were. Our choices are made in a setting of fundamental uncertainty. As such, basic attitudes toward human experience are at stake, and choices reflect overall interpretations of the lessons of history.

I am convinced that the renunciation of the nuclear option would serve national and world interests, principally by making nuclear war less likely to occur, by slowing the arms race, by inhibiting further proliferation of nuclear weapons, and by encouraging further steps toward positive disarmament. Beyond such expectations lies an awareness of the effects of using nuclear weapons and an understanding that a large-scale nuclear exchange will cause vast human (and ecological) damage to millions of innocent victims, many of whom may even oppose the governmental policy that provoked the nuclear attack, and will likely destroy or severely harm societies not even involved in the conflict. Such a weapon of limitless destruction is not reliably entrusted to the greeds and fears of human beings.

Whatever can be done to remove this awesome power from human control seems, on balance, beneficial. A renunciation of the nuclear option thus seems to be a clear step back from the edge of catastrophe, especially at this moment of history.

At the very least such a proposal warrants serious consideration by American policy-makers. So far, there has prevailed in the American elite a virtual consensus as to the national benefits derived from retaining the nuclear option. Such a consensus can only be explained as a consequence of excluding from power those who view the long history of deterrence of the weak by the strong as largely a costly failure even in the pre-nuclear years.

In conclusion, I would propose that the President recommend that Congress pass a joint resolution committing the United States to a renunciation of the nuclear option and that the President then declare this renunciation to the world as official policy. It would also be beneficial to join in a treaty rule confirming this renunciation. At minimum it is time to initiate a high-level public inquiry into the status of nuclear weapons and its effects upon national and world security. Both the President and the Congress should initiate studies of this issue and entrust the inquiry to civilians with no vested interest in nuclear technology. This kind of question should not be treated as a technical matter properly left within the province of professional military planners. The role of nuclear weapons in our defense posture should become primarily a matter for political judgment and moral appraisal.

Appendixes

A

Treaty on the
Non-Proliferation
of Nuclear Weapons

Treaty on the Non-Proliferation of Nuclear Weapons

The States concluding this Treaty, hereinafter referred to as the "Parties to the Treaty,"

Considering the devastation that would be visited upon all mankind by a nuclear war and the consequent need to make every effort to avert the danger of such a war and to take measures to safeguard the security of peoples,

Believing that the proliferation of nuclear weapons would seriously enhance the danger of nuclear war,

In conformity with resolutions of the United Nations General Assembly calling for the conclusion of an agreement on the prevention of wider dissemination of nuclear weapons,

Undertaking to cooperate in facilitating the application of International Atomic Energy Agency safeguards on peaceful nuclear activities,

Expressing their support for research, development and other efforts to further the application, within the framework of the International Atomic Energy Agency safeguards system, of the principle of safeguarding effectively the flow of source and special fissionable materials by use of instruments and other techniques at certain strategic points,

Affirming the principle that the benefits of peaceful applications of nuclear technology, including any technological by-products which may be derived by nuclear-weapon States from the development of nuclear explosive devices, should be available for peaceful purposes to all Parties to the Treaty, whether nuclear-weapon or non-nuclear-weapon States,

Convinced that, in furtherance of this principle, all Parties to the Treaty are entitled to participate in the fullest possible exchange of scientific information for, and to contribute alone or in cooperation with other States to, the further development of the   applications of atomic energy for peaceful purposes,

Declaring their intention to achieve at the earliest possible date the cessation of the nuclear arms race and to undertake effective measures in the direction of nuclear disarmament,

Urging the cooperation of all States in the attainment of this objective,

Recalling the determination expressed by the Parties to the 1963 Treaty banning nuclear weapon tests in the atmosphere in outer space and under water in its Preamble to seek to achieve the discontinuance of all test explosions of nuclear weapons for all time and to continue negotiations to this end,

Desiring to further the easing of international tension and the strengthening of trust between States in order to facilitate the cessation of the

U.N. Doc. A/7016/Add. 1; *Hearings on the Non-Proliferation Treaty*, 258-262.

manufacture of nuclear weapons, the liquidation of all their existing stockpiles, and the elimination from national arsenals of nuclear weapons and the means of their delivery pursuant to a treaty on general and complete disarmament under strict and effective international control.

Recalling that, in accordance with the Charter of the United Nations, States must refrain in their international relations from the threat or use of force against the territorial integrity or political independence of any State, or in any other manner inconsistent with the Purposes of the United Nations, and that the establishment and maintenance of international peace and security are to be promoted with the least diversion for armaments of the world's human and economic resources,

Have agreed as follows:

Article I

Each nuclear-weapon State Party to the Treaty undertakes not to transfer to any recipient whatsoever nuclear weapons or other nuclear explosive devices or control over such weapons or explosive devices or control over such weapons or explosive devices directly, or indirectly; and not in any way to assist, encourage, or induce any non-nuclear-weapon State to manufacture or otherwise acquire nuclear weapons or other nuclear explosive devices, or control over such weapons or explosive devices.

Article II

Each non-nuclear-weapon State Party to the Treaty undertakes not to receive the transfer from any transferor whatsoever of nuclear weapons or other nuclear explosive devices or of control over such weapons or explosive devices directly, or indirectly; not to manufacture or otherwise acquire nuclear weapons or other nuclear explosive devices; and not to seek or receive any assistance in the manufacture of nuclear weapons or other nuclear explosive devices.

Article III

1. Each non-nuclear-weapon State Party to the Treaty undertakes to accept safeguards, as set forth in an agreement to be negotiated and concluded with the International Atomic Energy Agency in accordance with the Statute of the International Atomic Energy Agency and the Agency's safeguards system, for the exclusive purpose of verification of the fulfillment of its obligations assumed under this Treaty with a view to preventing diversion of nuclear energy from peaceful uses to nuclear weapons or other nuclear explosive devices. Procedures for the safeguards required by this article shall be followed with respect to source or special fissionable material whether it is

being produced, processed or used in any principal nuclear facility or is outside any such facility. The safeguards required by this article shall be applied on all source or special fissionable material in all peaceful nuclear activities within the territory of such State, under its jurisdiction, or carried out under its control anywhere.

2. Each State Party to the Treaty undertakes not to provide: (a) source or special fissionable material, or (b) equipment or material especially designed or prepared for the processing, use or production of special fissionable material, to any non-nuclear-weapon State for peaceful purposes, unless the source or special fissionable material shall be subject to the safeguards required by this article.

3. The safeguards required by this article shall be implemented in a manner designed to comply with article IV of this Treaty, and to avoid hampering the economic or technological development of the Parties or international cooperation in the field of peaceful nuclear activities, including the international exchange of nuclear material and equipment for the processing, use or production of nuclear material for peaceful purposes in accordance with the provisions of this article and the principle of safeguarding set forth in the Preamble of the Treaty.

4. Non-nuclear-weapon States Party to the Treaty shall conclude agreements with the International Atomic Energy Agency to meet the requirements of this article either individually or together with other States in accordance with the Statute of the International Atomic Energy Agency. Negotiation of such agreements shall commence within 180 days from the original entry into force of this Treaty. For States depositing their instruments of ratification or accession after the 180-day period, negotiation of such agreements shall commence not later than the date of such deposit. Such agreements shall enter into force not later than eighteen months after the date of initiation of negotiations.

Article IV

1. Nothing in this Treaty shall be interpreted as affecting the inalienable right of all the Parties to the Treaty to develop research, production and use of nuclear energy for peaceful purposes without discrimination and in conformity with articles I and II of this Treaty.

2. All the Parties to the Treaty undertake to facilitate, and have the right to participate in, the fullest possible exchange of equipment, materials and scientific and technological information for the peaceful uses of nuclear energy. Parties to the Treaty in a position to do so shall also cooperate in contributing alone or together with other States or international organiza-

tions to the further development of the applications of nuclear energy for peaceful purposes, especially in the territories of non-nuclear-weapon States Party to the Treaty, with due consideration for the needs of the developing areas of the world.

Article V

Each Party to the Treaty undertakes to take appropriate measures to ensure that, in accordance with this Treaty, under appropriate international observation and through appropriate international procedures, potential benefits from any peaceful applications of nuclear explosions will be made available to non-nuclear-weapon States Party to the Treaty on a non-discriminatory basis and that the charge to such Parties for the explosive devices used will be as low as possible and exclude any charge for research and development. Non-nuclear-weapon States Party to the Treaty shall be able to obtain such benefits, pursuant to a special international agreement or agreements, through an appropriate international body with adequate representation of non-nuclear-weapon States. Negotiations on this subject shall commence as soon as possible after the Treaty enters into force. Non-nuclear-weapon States Party to the Treaty so desiring may also obtain such benefits pursuant to bilateral agreements.

Article VI

Each of the Parties to the Treaty undertakes to pursue negotiations in good faith on effective measures relating to cessation of the nuclear arms race at an early date and to nuclear disarmament, and on a treaty on general and complete disarmament under strict and effective international control.

Article VII

Nothing in this Treaty affects the right of any group of States to conclude regional treaties in order to assure the total absence of nuclear weapons in their respective territories.

Article VIII

1. Any Party to the Treaty may propose amendments to this Treaty. The text of any proposed amendment shall be submitted to the Depositary Governments which shall circulate it to all Parties to the Treaty. Thereupon, if requested to do so by one-third or more of the Parties to the Treaty, the Depositary Governments shall convene a conference, to which they shall invite all the Parties to the Treaty, to consider such an amendment.

2. Any amendment to this Treaty must be approved by a majority of the votes of all the Parties to the Treaty, including the votes of all nuclear-weapon States Party to the Treaty and all other Parties which, on the date the amendment is circulated, are members of the Board of Governors of the International Atomic Energy Agency. The amendment shall enter into force for each Party that deposits its instrument of ratification of the amendment upon the deposit of such instruments of ratification by a majority of all the Parties, including the instruments of ratification of all nuclear-weapon States Party to the Treaty and all other Parties which, on the date the amendment is circulated, are members of the Board of Governors of the International Atomic Energy Agency. Thereafter, it shall enter into force for any other Party upon the deposit of its instrument of ratification of the amendment.

3. Five years after the entry into force of this Treaty, a conference of Parties to the Treaty shall be held in Geneva, Switzerland, in order to review the operation of this Treaty with a view to assuring that the purposes of the Preamble and the provisions of the Treaty are being realized. At intervals of five years thereafter, a majority of the Parties to the Treaty may obtain, by submitting a proposal to this effect to the Depositary Governments, the convening of further conferences with the same objective of reviewing the operation of the Treaty.

Article IX

1. This Treaty shall be open to all States for signature. Any State which does not sign the Treaty before its entry into force in accordance with paragraph 3 of this article may accede to it at any time.

2. This Treaty shall be subject to ratification by signatory States. Instruments of ratification and instruments of accession shall be deposited with the Governments of the United States of America, the United Kingdom of Great Britain and Northern Ireland and the Union of Soviet Socialist Republics, which are hereby designated the Depositary Governments.

3. This Treaty shall enter into force after its ratification by the States, the Governments of which are designated Depositaries of the Treaty, and forty other States signatory to this Treaty and the deposit of their instruments of ratification. For the purposes of this Treaty, a nuclear-weapon State is one which has manufactured and exploded a nuclear weapon or other nuclear explosive device prior to January 1, 1967.

4. For States whose instruments of ratification or accession are deposited subsequent to the entry into force of this Treaty, it shall enter into force on the date of the deposit of their instruments of ratification or accession.

5. The Depositary Governments shall promptly inform all signatory and acceding States of the date of each signature, the date of deposit of each

instrument of ratification or of accession, the date of the entry into force of this Treaty, and the date of receipt of any requests for convening a conference or other notices.

6. This Treaty shall be registered by the Depositary Governments pursuant to article 102 of the Charter of the United Nations.

Article X

1. Each Party shall in exercising its national sovereignty have the right to withdraw from the Treaty if it decides that extraordinary events, related to the Subject matter of this Treaty, have jeopardized the supreme interests of its country. It shall give notice of such withdrawal to all other Parties to the Treaty and to the United Nations Security Council three months in advance. Such notice shall include a statement of the extraordinary events it regards as having jeopardized its supreme interests.

2. Twenty-five years after the entry into force of the Treaty, a conference shall be convened to decide whether the Treaty shall continue in force indefinitely, or shall be extended for an additional fixed period or periods. This decision shall be taken by a majority of the Parties to the Treaty.

Article XI

This Treaty, the English, Russian, French, Spanish and Chinese texts of which are equally authentic, shall be deposited in the archives of the Depositary Governments. Duly certified copies of this Treaty shall be transmitted by the Depositary Governments to the Governments of the signatory and acceding States.

IN WITNESS WHEREOF the undersigned, duly authorized, have signed this Treaty.

DONE in triplicate, at the cities of Washington, London and Moscow, this first day of   July one thousand nine hundred sixty-eight.

B   United Nations Security Council Resolution on Security Assurances

United Nations Security Council
Resolution on Security Assurances

The Security Council

Noting with appreciation the desire of a large number of States to subscribe to the Treaty on the Non-Proliferation of Nuclear Weapons, and thereby to undertake not to receive the transfer from any transferor whatsoever of nuclear weapons or other nuclear explosive devices or of control over such weapons or explosive devices directly, or indirectly; not to manufacture or otherwise acquire nuclear weapons or other nuclear explosive devices; and not to seek or receive any assistance in the manufacture of nuclear weapons or other nuclear explosive devices,

Taking into consideration the concern of certain of these States that, in conjunction with their adherence to the Treaty on the Non-Proliferation of Nuclear Weapons, appropriate measures be undertaken to safeguard their security,

Bearing in mind that any aggression accompanied by the use of nuclear weapons would endanger the peace and security of all States,

1. *Recognizes* that aggression with nuclear weapons or the threat of such aggression against a non-nuclear-weapon State would create a situation in which the Security Council, and above all its nuclear-weapon State permanent members, would have to act immediately in accordance with their obligations under the United Nations Charter;

2. *Welcomes* the intention expressed by certain States that they will provide or support immediate assistance, in accordance with the Charter, to any non-nuclear-weapon State Party to the Treaty on the Non-Proliferation of Nuclear Weapons that is a victim of an act or an object of a threat of aggression in which nuclear weapons are used;

3. *Reaffirms* in particular the inherent right, recognized under Article 51 of the Charter, of individual and collective self-defense if an armed attack occurs against a Member of the United Nations, until the Security Council has taken measures necessary to maintain international peace and security.

Adopted by the Security Council at its 1433rd meeting on June 19, 1968, S/RES/255, 1968.

C   Declaration of the Government of the United States of America

Declaration of the Government of the United States of America

The Government of the United States notes with appreciation the desire expressed by a large number of States to subscribe to the treaty on the non-proliferation of nuclear weapons.

We welcome the willingness of these States to undertake not to receive the transfer from any transferor whatsoever of nuclear weapons or other nuclear explosive devices or of control over such weapons or explosive devices directly, or indirectly; not to manufacture or otherwise acquire nuclear weapons or other nuclear explosive devices; and not to seek or receive any assistance in the manufacture of nuclear weapons or other nuclear explosive devices.

The United States also notes the concern of certain of these States that, in conjunction with their adherence to the treaty on the non-proliferation of nuclear weapons, appropriate measures be undertaken to safeguard their security. Any aggression accompanied by the use of nuclear weapons would endanger the peace and security of all States.

Bearing these considerations in mind, the United States declares the following:

Aggression with nuclear weapons, or the threat of such aggression, against a non-nuclear-weapon State would create a qualitatively new situation in which the nuclear-weapon States which are permanent members of the United Nations Security Council would have to act immediately through the Security Council to take the measures necessary to counter such aggression or to remove the threat of aggression in accordance with the United Nations Charter, which calls for taking "* * *effective collective measures for the prevention and removal of threats to the peace, and for the suppression of acts of aggression or other breaches of the peace * * *". Therefore, any State which commits aggression accompanied by the use of nuclear weapons or which threatens such aggression must be aware .that its actions are to be countered effectively by measures to be taken in accordance with the United Nations Charter to suppress the aggression or remove the threat of aggression.

The United States affirms its intention, as a permanent member of the United Nations Security Council, to seek immediate Security Council action to provide assistance, in accordance with the Charter, to any non-nuclear-weapon State party to the treaty on the non-proliferation of nuclear weapons that is a victim of an act of aggression or an object of a threat of aggression in which nuclear weapons are used.

Made in the United Nations Security Council at its 1430th meeting on July 17, 1968, in explanation of its vote for Security Council Resolution 255 (1968).

163

The United States reaffirms in particular the inherent right, recognized under Article 51 of the Charter, of individual and collective self-defense if an armed attack, including a nuclear attack, occurs against a Member of the United Nations, until the Security Council has taken measures necessary to maintain international peace and security.

The United States vote for the resolution before us and this statement of the way in which the United States intends to act in accordance with the Charter of the United Nations are based upon the fact that the resolution is supported by other permanent members of the Security Council which are nuclear-weapon States and are also proposing to sign the treaty on the non-proliferation of nuclear weapons, and that these States have made similar statements as to the way in which they intend to act in accordance with the Charter.

D   Signatures and Accessions to the Treaty

Signatures and Accessions to the Treaty

Treaty on the Non-Proliferation of Nuclear Weapons Opened for Signature at Washington, London, and Moscow on July 1, 1968. Entered into Force on March 5, 1970

Signature at Washington, and on July 1, 1968, unless otherwise indicated. States that have deposited their instruments of ratification are underlined, and the date of deposit is indicated in parenthesis.*

Afghanistan - (2/4/70)
Australia - 2/27/70
Austria (6/27/69)
Barbados
Belgium - 8/20/68
Bolivia
Botswana (4/28/69) (L)**
Bulgaria (9/5/69)
Cameroon - 7/17/68 (1/8/69)
Canada - 7/23/68 (1/8/69)
Ceylon
Chad (M)**
China, Rep. of (1/27/70)
Colombia
Congo (Kinshasa) - 7/22/68
Costa Rica (3/3/70)
Cyprus (2/10/70)
Czechoslovakia (7/22/69)
Dahomey
Denmark (1/3/69)
Dominican Republic
Ecuador - 7/9/68 (3/7/69)
El Salvador
Ethiopia - 9/5/68 (2/5/70)
Finland (2/5/69)
Gambia - 9/20/68
Germany, Fed. Rep. of - 11/28/69
Ghana
Greece (3/11/70)
Guatemala - 7/26/68

Haiti
Honduras
Hungary (5/27/69)
Iceland (7/18/69)
Indonesia - 3/2/70
Iran (2/2/70)
Iraq (M)**(10/29/69) (M)**
Ireland (7/1/68)
Italy - 1/28/69
Ivory Coast
Jamaica - 4/14/69 (3/5/70)
Japan - 2/3/70
Jordan - 7/10/68 (2/11/70)
Kenya
Korea, Rep. of
Kuwait - 8/15/68
Laos (2/20/70)
Lebanon
Lesotho - 7/9/68
Liberia (3/5/70)
Libya - 7/19/68
Luxembourg - 8/14/68
Malagasy Republic - 8/22/68
Malaysia (3/5/70)
Maldive Islands - 9/11/68
Mali - 7/14/69 (2/10/70)
Malta - 4/17/69 (2/6/70)
Mauritius (4/8/69)
Mexico - 7/26/68 (1/21/69)
Mongolia (M)** (5/14/69) (M)**

*The United States has not accepted notification of the signature, nor of the deposit of ratification instrument, in Moscow, of the German Democratic Republic.

**Denotes place of signature (or, if after parenthesized date, deposit) as follows:

(M)   in Moscow only
(L)   in London only
(ML)   in Moscow and London
TOTALS: 97 Signatures (88 of which were in Washington, D.C.)
             49 Deposits (44 of which were in Washington, D.C.)

Morocco
Nepal (1/5/70)
Netherlands - 8/20/68
New Zealand (9/10/69)
Nicaragua
Nigeria (10/7/68)
Norway (2/5/69)
Panama
Paraguay (2/4/70)
Peru (3/3/70)
Philippines
Poland (6/12/69)
Romania (2/4/70)
San Marino
Senegal
Singapore - 2/5/70
Somali Republic (3/5/70)
Southern Yemen - 11/14/68 (M)**
Sudan - 12/24/68 (M)**

Swaziland - 6/24/69 (L)**(12/16/69)
Sweden - 8/19/68 (1/9/70)
Switzerland - 11/27/69
Syria (M)** (9/24/69) (M)**
Togo - (2/26/70)
Trinidad & Tobago - 8/20/68
Tunisia (2/26/70)
Turkey - 1/28/69
UAR (M-L)**
UK (11/27/68)
USA (3/5/70)
USSR (3/5/70)
Upper Volta - 11/25/68 (3/3/70)
Uruguay
Venezuela
Viet Nam, Rep. of
Yemen Arab Rep. - 9/23/68 (M)**
Yugoslavia - 7/10/68 (3/4/70)

E American Society
of International
Law
Panel on Nuclear
Energy and World
Order

171

Notes

Notes to Chapter 3

(All *Documents on Disarmament* cited below can be obtained from the Government Printing Office, Washington, D.C.)

1. A list of those countries that had signed and those that had ratified when the treaty entered into force appears as Appendix D.

2. A list of those countries that have ratified appears in Appendix D.

3. *Hearings on Executive H* (The Non-Proliferation Treaty), before the Senate Committee on Foreign Relations, 90th Congress, 1st and 2nd Sessions (Part 1, 1968), pp. 30-31; *Hearing on the Military Implications of the Treaty on the Non-Proliferation of Nuclear Weapons,* before the Senate Committee on Armed Services, 91st Congress, 1st Session (1969), p. 96.

4. *Ibid.*

5. Austria, Belgium, Czechoslovakia, Hungary, the Netherlands, Poland, Switzerland, the United Arab Republic, and Yugoslavia have signed. Austria, Czechoslovakia, Hungary, Poland, and Yugoslavia have also ratified. See Appendix D.

6. Argentina, Brazil, and Chile. For texts, see Treaty on the Prohibition of Nuclear Weapons in Latin America, *Documents on Disarmament, 1967,* p. 69; *Documents on Disarmament, 1968,* pp. 203-205.

7. *Hearings on Executive H, op. cit.* (Part 2, 1969), p. 336

8. The treaty appears at Appendix A.

9. *Hearings on Executive H, op. cit.* (Part 1, 1968), p. 39; Mason Willrich, *Non-Proliferation Treaty: Framework for Nuclear Arms Control* (Charlottesville: Michie, 1969), p. 93.

10. *Ibid.*

11. Lord Chalfont, quoted in George Bunn, *"The Nuclear Nonproliferation Treaty," Wisconsin Law Review* (1968), pp. 766, 772. For discussion of the undertaking by the nuclear parties to make any potential benefits of peaceful applications of nuclear explosive devices available to non-nuclear parties, see Bernhard G. Bechhoefer, "Plowshare Control," in this volume.

12. Bunn, *ibid.,* pp. 778-779.

13. *Hearings on Executive H. op. cit.,*pp. 5-6; *Hearings on the Military Implications, op. cit.,* pp. 11-12.

14. The arrangements the Soviet Union has with its Warsaw Pact allies are thought to involve even less proximity of non-nuclear country personnel to

nuclear weapons than those of the United States. Although these arrangements are not as well known to the United States as those of NATO are to the Soviet Union because of the differences in "openness" and freedom of the press, present Soviet arrangements are believed to comply with the treaty. And the treaty provides a good reason for the Soviets to say No to their allies if, as is likely, they do not wish to give non-nuclear countries nuclear weapons or information on how to make them.

15. Bunn, *op. cit.*, pp. 769-771.

16. *Ibid.* p. 779.

17. *Hearings on Executive H., op. cit.*, p. 340; *Hearings on Military Implications, op. cit.* p. 123.

18. Address by President Johnson at Seattle, September 16, 1964, *Documents on Disarmament, 1964*, p. 431.

19. *Hearings on Executive H, op. cit.*, p. 357.

20. *The New York Times*, November 13, 1968, Sec. 1, p. 3, col. 3.

21. See *Treaty on the Nonproliferation of Nuclear Weapons*, Exec. Rep. No. 9, Senate Committee on Foreign Relations (1968), p. 12.

22. *Hearings on Executive H, op. cit.*, pp. 263-264.

23. *Ibid.*, pp. 424-425.

Notes to Chapter 4

1. These are convenient multiples of 5 kg near the critical masses at normal densities. Precise figures for a large number of cases are given in H. C. Paxton, *Los Alamos Critical-Mass Data*, Report LAMS-3067 (Los Alamos Scientific Laboratory, May 6, 1964) (Unclassified).

2. Since the necessary critical mass *decreases* as the material density increases. See the item "Weapons (Nuclear)" in J. F. Hogerton, *The Atomic Energy Deskbook* (New York: Reinhold Publishing Company, 1963).

3. *Nuclear Industry* (November 1969), p. 21.

4. See "Terms Agreed on Three-Nation Centrifuge Plans," *Nuclear Engineering International* (February 1970), p. 74.

5. See "European Centrifuge Partners Will Sell Enrichment Technology," *Nucleonics Week* (December 25, 1969).

6. Those interested in technical details of enrichment should see *Gaseous Diffusion Plant Operations*, U.S. AEC ORO-658 (February 1968).

7. *Nuclear Industry* (September 1969) p. 32.

8. Mason Willrich, *Non-Proliferation Treaty: Framework for Nuclear Arms Control* (Charlottesville: Michie, 1969), p. 93.

Notes to Chapter 5

1. Atomic Industrial Forum, Subcommittee on Fuel Fabrication Plant Safeguards, D. J. Povejsil, Chairman, *Fuel Fabrication Plant Safeguards* (November 26, 1969).

Notes to Chapter 8

1. Most literature on the subject of non-military uses of nuclear explosives is concerned with technical feasibility. A small fraction is concerned with the economic aspects of the various proposals. Of that literature concerned with the economic aspects, the most extensive discussion of cost-benefit considerations is found in the monograph entitled "Peaceful Uses of Nuclear Explosives," by Brooks and Krutilla (Baltimore: Johns Hopkins University Press, 1969).

2. *Ibid.* On pp. 22-23, Brooks and Krutilla refer to Robert H. Haveman, *Water Resource Investment and the Public Interest* (Nashville: Vanderbilt University Press, 1965), Appendix B.

3. JCAE Hearings, *Nuclear Explosion Services for Industrial Applications* (1969), p. 707.

4. *World Oil* (Gulf Publishing Co., September-October 1969).

5. Coffer *et al.* noted this in a paper prepared for the Fourth Plowshare Symposium (Las Vegas, Nevada, January 1970).

6. Ketch Proposal, *Columbia Gas System* (July 1967), p. 7.

7. JCAE Hearings, *AEC Authorizing Legislation* (Fiscal Year 1970), p. 333.

8. JCAE Hearings, *Commercial Plowshare Services* (July 1968), pp. 123-166.

9. JCAE Hearings, *AEC Authorizing Legislation* (Fiscal Year 1970), p. 318. A second meeting was held in Moscow in February, 1970, and further meetings are expected in the future.

10. JCAE Hearings, *Nuclear Explosion Services for Industrial Applications* (1969), pp. 272-313.

Notes to Chapter 9

(All *Documents on Disarmament* cited below can be obtained from the Government Printing Office, Washington, D.C.)

1. Statement of Dr. Glenn T. Seaborg, AEC Chairman (January 5, 1965), in U.S. Congress, Joint Committee on Atomic Energy, *Hearing on Peaceful Applications of Nuclear Explosives-Plowshare* (89th Congress, 1st Session), p. 2.

2. Klaus Knorr, "Curbing Nuclear Proliferation," address to Canadian-American Assembly on Nuclear Weapons, Scarborough, Canada, June 15, 1967, p. 9. (Unpublished.)

3. For the entire text of Article V, see Appendix A.

4. UN General Assembly Resolution 2456C (XXIII).

5. For example, "IAEA with its present structure already has the necessary possibilities for undertaking tasks relating to the use of nuclear explosions for peaceful purposes in accordance with the Treaty. In our view, therefore, there is no need to establish a special IAEA service for nuclear explosions for peaceful purposes, separate from the departments already existing in the Agency" (U.S.S.R. Comments, UN Document A/7678, September 29, 1969, p. 36). The United Kingdom (U.K. Comments, UN Document A/7678, September 29, 1969, p. 37) and the United States (U.S. Comments, UN Document A/7678, September 29, 1969, pp. 38-39) expressed similar views.
The United States supported the concept that the IAEA organization should be kept "under periodic review to assure that it will be able to meet its responsibilities in the field of peaceful nuclear explosions."

6. UN Document A/Conf 35/Doc 15, Geneva (August 22, 1968).

7. Comments of Jamaica, UN Document A/7678 (September 29, 1969), p. 24.

8. UN Document A/7678, pp. 43-46.

9. For generally parallel list of functions, see Ulf Ericcson, "The Question of Nuclear Explosions for Peaceful Purposes by Non-nuclear-weapons States and the Possibility of Misuse of Such Technology for the Production of Nuclear Weapons," UN Document A/Conf 35/Doc 3 (July 3, 1968), pp. 5, 6.

10. Comments of Sweden, UN Document A/7678 (September 29, 1969), p. 33.

11. UN Document A/7678, p. 36.

12. UN Document A/Conf 35/Doc 15, Annex, pp. 9, 13.

13. UN Document A/7678, p. 39.

14. State Department answer to Question 6 by Senator Cooper in U.S. Congress (July 10, 1968), Senate Committee on Foreign Relations, *Hearings on Nonproliferation Treaty* (90th Congress, 2nd Session), pp. 50-51.

15. UN Document A/7678, p. 43.

16. UN Document A/7678, pp. 36, 37.

17. *Documents on Disarmament, 1961*, p. 98, Article 13.

18. U.S. Congress (90th Congress, 2nd Session), Joint Committee on Atomic Energy, Subcommittee on Legislation, *Hearings on Commercial Plowshare Services* (July 19, 1968), pp. 7-8.

19. *Documents on Disarmament, 1961.*

20. *Documents on Disarmament, 1961.*

21. David W. Wainhouse *et al., Arms Control Agreements* (Baltimore: Johns Hopkins University Press, 1968), p. 109.

22. Harold Jacobson and Eric Stein, *Diplomats, Scientists and Politicians* (Ann Arbor: University of Michigan Press, 1966), p. 271.

23. Statement of Ambassador Fisher to ENDC, August 9, 1969, *Documents on Disarmament, 1966*, p. 521.

24. *Documents on Disarmament, 1967*, pp. 69-83.

25. *Ibid.*, Article 12.

26. *Ibid.*, Article 18.

27. Principles Relating to Nuclear Explosion Services suggested by U.S. representative to ENDC, March 21, 1967, reprinted in *Hearings on Nonproliferation Treaty, op. cit.*, p. 12; statement of Secretary of State Senate Committee, p. 22; statement of Kuznetsov to First Committee G.A., May 20, 1968, reprinted in *Documents on Disarmament, 1968*, p. 375.

28. Mason Willrich, *Non-Proliferation Treaty: Framework for Nuclear Arms Control* (Charlottesville: Michie, 1969), p. 218.

29. *Ibid.*, pp. 147, 148.

30. *Hearings on Commerical Plowshare Services, op. cit.*, p. 15.

31. UN Document A/7678, p. 37.

32. Ericcson, *op. cit.*, p. 13.

33. William C. Foster, "Unfinished Business," address at Airlie House, Warrenton, Va., October 9, 1969 (unpublished). The non-nuclear weapon states in the ENDC, generally spearheaded by Sweden, have consistently advocated such a step and have obtained United Nations General Assembly resolutions to the same effect. It may be significant that William C. Foster, former director of the U.S. Arms Control and Disarmament Agency, in his first public statement after his retirement, likewise favored such a development even without intrusive inspection behind the Iron Curtain. He justifies his position on the ground that the danger to the world of undetected underground nuclear explosions today is less than the danger of military escalation through continued unlimited underground explosions. To quote Klaus Knorr *op. cit.*, on this subject:

> If a strong anti-proliferation treaty is established, a more restrictive nuclear test ban will probably be next on the agenda of those pressing for internationally comprehensive measures of nuclear arms control. The nascent Plowshare technology has a direct bearing on this matter. A nuclear test ban as absolutely as prohibitive as envisioned some years ago would obviously do away with all underground nuclear explosions and hence bury the Plowshare technology. Given the current spread of interest in this technology, a complete ban on nuclear explosions would scarcely seem feasible. Indeed, it would be the logic of any provisions for Plowshare-type explosions in an anti-proliferation treaty that "peaceful" explosions be exempted from a nuclear test ban.

34. *"Five Principles,"* March 21, 1967, reprinted in *Hearings on Commercial Plowshare Services, op. cit.*, p. 14; statement of Secretary of State to Foreign Relations Committee, *Hearings on Non-Proliferation Treaty, op. cit.*, p. 22, and statement of Chairman Seaborg, *op. cit.*, p. 16; statement of Kuznetsov to first Committee of General Assembly, May 20, 1968, reprinted in *Documents on Disarmament, 1968*, p. 375.

35. Foster, *op. cit.*

36. Ericcson, *op. cit.*

37. *The Atom* (Los Alamos Scientific Laboratory: October, 1969).

38. Statement of Dr. Tape, *Hearings on Commercial Plowshare Services, op. cit.*, p. 16.

39. Statement of John S. Kelley, AEC on Plowshare Program, *Peaceful Applications of Nuclear Explosives-Plowshare, op. cit.*, p. 35.

40. Statement of Chairman Seaborg, *ibid.*, p. 2.

Notes on Chapter 10

1. For example, a Swedish study showed that an attack with some 200 comparatively small weapons (20-200 kilotons in yield) would kill 30-40 percent of the population of Sweden and destroy 30-70 percent of its industry. United Nations Report A/6858, *Effects of the Possible Use of Nuclear Weapons and the Security and Economic Implications for States of the Acquisition and Further Development of These Weapons* (New York, 1968), p. 13.

2. U.S. Congress, Joint Committee on Atomic Energy, *Non-Proliferation of Nuclear Weapons*, p. 12, quoted in William B. Bader, *The United States and the Spread of Nuclear Weapons* (New York: Pegasus Books, 1968), p. 110.

3. United Nations Security Council Resolution 255, of June 19, 1968, for which these three countries voted:

1) *Recognizes* that aggression with nuclear weapons or the threat of such aggression against a non-nuclear-weapon State would create a situation in which the Security Council, and above all its nuclear-weapon State Permanent Members, would have to act immediately in accordance with their obligations under the United Nations Charter; [and]

2) *Welcomes* the intention expressed by certain states that they will provide or support immediate assistance, in accordance with the Charter, to any non-nuclear-weapon State party to the treaty on the Nonproliferation of Nuclear Weapons that is a victim of an act or an object of a threat of aggression in which nuclear weapons are used. . . .

For the complete text of the Resolution, see *The New York Times* (June 18, 1968), p. 2, cols. 4 and 5.

4. France, although separately indicating its willingness ". . . to go to the assistance of any non-nuclear nation that was threatened with nuclear aggression," abstained from voting on Resolution 255, and has indicated that it will not sign the Non-Proliferation Treaty.

5. The operative paragraphs of the U.S. declaration preceding the Security Council vote were:

Aggression with nuclear weapons, or the threat of such aggression, against a non-nuclear weapons State would create a qualitatively new situation in which the nuclear weapons states that are permanent members of the Security Council would have to act immediately through the Security Council to take the measures necessary to counter such aggression or to remove the threat of such aggression in accordance with the United Nations Charter, which calls for taking "effective collective measures for the prevention and removal of threats to the peace and for the suppression of acts of aggression or other breaches of the peace."

The United States affirms its intention, as a permanent member of the United Nations Security Council, to seek immediate Security Council action to provide assistance, in accordance with the Charter, to any non-nuclear-weapons state party to the treaty on the Nonproliferation of Nuclear Weapons that is a victim of an act of aggression or an object of a threat of aggression in which nuclear weapons are used.

The United States vote for the resolution before us, and this statement of the way in which the United States intends to act in accordance with the Charter of the United Nations, are based upon the fact that the resolution is supported by other permanent members of the [Security] Council who are nuclear-weapons states and are also proposing to sign the Treaty on the Nonproliferation of Nuclear Weapons, and that these states have made similar statements as to the way in which they intend to act in accordance with the Charter.

The New York Times (June 18, 1968), p. 2, cols. 4-5.

6. *The New York Times* (July 11, 1968), p. 16, col. 3.

7. It is conceivable that Czechoslovakia and East Germany could feel so threatened by the United States and its allies that they would consider the development of nuclear weapons; however, even if this were the case, the constraints on such development are so great as to make it extremely unlikely. Moreover, it is difficult to see what U.S. measures (short of a complete reversal of its current policies toward Europe) could alleviate such fears, should they in fact arise.

8. For a more detailed discussion of these points, see J. I. Coffey, "Strategy, Alliance Policy, and Nuclear Proliferation," *Orbis*, Vol. XI, No. 4 (Winter, 1968), esp. pp. 992-995.

9. *The New York Times* (October 27, 1969), p. 19, col. 1.

Notes to Chapter 11

(All *Documents on Disarmament* cited below can be obtained from the Government Printing Office, Washington, D.C.)

1. Interview between Premier Khrushchev and C. S. Sulzberger, September 5, 1961, *Documents on Disarmament, 1961,* pp. 355-360, at p. 358; statement of Nikita S. Khrushchev, Prime Minister of the Soviet Union: "We are maintaining our rockets armed with the most powerful thermonuclear weapons in constant combat readiness, *but the Soviet Union will never be the*

first to set these weapons in motion and unleash a world war." The New York Times, July 20, 1963, p. 2 (emphasis supplied); Chinese Communist communique on hydrogen bomb test, December 28, 1968: "The Chinese Communist Government reiterates once again that the conducting of necessary and limited nuclear tests and the development of nuclear weapons by China are entirely for the purpose of defense and for breaking the nuclear monopoly, with the ultimate aim of abolishing nuclear weapons. We solemnly declare once again that at no time and in no circumstances will China be the first to use nuclear weapons. We always mean what we say." *Documents on Disarmament, 1968,* pp. 808-810.

2. *Documents on Disarmament, 1967,* pp. 420-421.

3. The most important development in this direction is the 1967 Treaty for the Prohibition of Nuclear Weapons in Latin America—the Treaty of Tlatelolco—which has been signed by twenty-one Latin American countries. See Mason Willrich, *Non-Proliferation Treaty: Framework for Nuclear Control* (Charlottesville: Michie, 1969), pp. 55-57, for a brief discussion of the characteristics of this treaty.

4. *Documents on Disarmament, 1961,* pp. 648-650.

5. For example, G.A. Res. 1909 (XVIII) calling upon the Eighteen Nation Committee on Disarmament to convene a conference for the purpose of signing a treaty of prohibition was supported by a vote of 64-18-25, *Documents on Disarmament, 1963,* p. 626; and G.A. Res. 2289 (XXII), passed by a vote of 77-0-29, urges all states to consider, in light of G.A. Res. 1653, signing a draft convention on the prohibition of nuclear weapons submitted by the Soviet Union, *Documents on Disarmament, 1967,* pp. 626-627.

6. See, in particular, Report to Secretary General U Thant by a group of consultant experts on the Effects of Possible Use of Nuclear Weapons, *Documents on Disarmament, 1967,* pp. 476-513.

7. For discussion of these issues see Richard A. Falk, *The Status of Law in International Society* (Princeton: Princeton University Press, 1970), pp. 174-184. See also Jorge Castañeda, *Legal Effects of United Nations Resolutions* (New York: Columbia University Press, 1969); and Obed Y. Asamoah, *The Legal Significance of the Declarations of the General Assembly of the United Nations* (The Hague: Martinus Nijhoff, 1966).

8. Among the literature about the legality of nuclear weapons see Georg Schwarzenberger, *The Legality of Nuclear Weapons* (London: Stevens and Sons, 1958); Nagendra Singh, *Nuclear Weapons and International Law* (New York: Praeger, 1959); Myres S. McDougal and Florentino P. Feliciano, *Law and Minimum World Public Order: The Legal Regulation of International Coercion* (New Haven: Yale University Press, 1961); and William V. O'Brien, *War and/or Survival* (Garden City: Doubleday, 1969), especially pp. 108-130. See also *Shimoda* decision cited and described in text at note 20 below.

9. Department of the Army Field Manual, FM 27-10, *The Law of Land Warfare* (July 1956), paragraph 35, p. 18, on Atomic Weapons, cited in full, states:

> The use of explosive "atomic weapons," whether by air, sea, or land forces, cannot as such be regarded as violative of international law in the absence of any customary rule of international law or international convention restricting their employment.

The Law of Naval Warfare, in Robert W. Tucker, *The Law of War and Neutrality at Sea* (U.S. Naval War College, International Law Studies, 1955), pp. 358-422, Article 613 on Nuclear Weapons, at p. 410, cited in full, states:

> There is at present no rule of international law expressly prohibiting states from the use of nuclear weapons in warfare. In the absence of express prohibition, the use of such weapons against enemy combatants and other military objectives is permitted.

Footnote 9, on p. 416, adds that, in effect, nuclear bombs are subject to the same laws as are conventional bombs, and U.S. forces may use nuclear weapons only on direction from the President.

10. See William Brecher, "NATO Planners Move Toward Greater Stress on Atomic Weapons," *The New York Times* (November 13, 1969), p.8.

11. Bernard Brodie, *Escalation and Nuclear Option* (Princeton: Princeton University Press, 1966), pp. 132-33.

12. *Documents on Disarmament, 1967,* p. 588.

13. *Ibid.* cf. language on p. 588.

14. *Ibid.* p. 589.

15. For one exposition of this judgment see Edward Teller and Allen Brown, *The Legacy of Hiroshima* (Garden City: Doubleday, 1962).

16. *Department of State Bulletin,* January 12, 1954.

17. Brodie, *op. cit.,* p. 4.

18. For text, see Richard A. Falk and Saul H. Mendlovitz, eds., *The Strategy of World Order* (New York: World Law Fund, 1966), III, pp. 280-282.

19. Thomas B. Larson, *Disarmament and Soviet Policy, 1964-1968* (Englewood Cliffs, New Jersey: Prentice-Hall, 1969), p. 167.

20. For text, see Falk and Mendlovitz, *ibid.,* I, pp. 314-354; for discussion see Richard A. Falk, *Legal Order in a Violent World* (Princeton University Press, 1968), pp. 374-413.

21. *Documents on Disarmament, 1967,* p. 593.

22. *Documents on Disarmament, 1967,* p. 580.

23. This observation is well documented in Ralph K. White, *Nobody Wanted War* (rev. ed.; Garden City: Doubleday Anchor, 1970).

24. I am indebted to Harold Feiveson for the ideas embodied in this paragraph.

25. *The New York Times* (November 26, 1969), p. 16.

26. I am indebted to Harold Feiveson for the ideas embodied in this paragraph.

About the Editors

BENNETT BOSKEY is engaged in the private practice of law in Washington, D.C. He has written on the Supreme Court and on various aspects of atomic energy matters. Mr. Boskey is a former Deputy General Counsel of the United States Atomic Energy Commission.

MASON WILLRICH is Professor of Law and Director of the Center for the Study of Science, Technology and Public Policy at the University of Virginia. His publications include a recent book, *Non-Proliferation Treaty: Framework for Nuclear Arms Control* (Charlottesville: Michie, 1969), and numerous articles. He was formerly Assistant General Counsel, U.S. Arms Control and Disarmament Agency.

About the Contributors

Bernhard G. Bechhoefer, an attorney practicing in Washington, D.C., is a graduate of Harvard College and holds an L.L.B. degree from Harvard Law School. Mr. Bechhoefer served as a consultant to the Brookings Institution from 1959 to 1969. He is the co-author of *Arms Control Agreements* (1968).

David B. Brooks, Chief of the Division of Mineral Economics in the Bureau of Mines, U.S. Department of the Interior, received his Ph.D. degree in Economics from the University of Colorado. Mr. Brooks spent several years with the U.S. Geological Survey in Western United States and with Economics for the Future, Inc., prior to assuming his present position. He is the co-author of *Peaceful Use of Nuclear Explosives: Some Economic Aspects* (1969).

George Bunn is Professor of Law at the University of Wisconsin. He was General Counsel for the U.S. Arms Control and Disarmament Agency and lawyer-member of the U.S. Delegation to the Geneva Disarmament Conference or Deputy Chairman of the Delegation during the negotiation of the Non-Proliferation Treaty. In these capacities, he helped draft and negotiate the treaty.

Joseph I. Coffey, Professor of Public and International Affairs at the Graduate School of Public and International Affairs, Pittsburgh University, received his Ph.D. degree in International Relations from Georgetown University. Mr. Coffey served as Chief, Office of National Security Studies, with the Bendix Systems Division from 1963 to 1967. He is the co-author of *The Presidential Staff* (1961).

Richard A. Falk is Albert G. Milbank Professor of International Law and Practice at Princeton University. His books include *Legal Order in a Violent World* (1968) and *The Status of Law in International Society* (1970), and he edited, with Richard J. Barnet, *Security in Disarmament* (1965). Professor Falk is Vice-President of the American Society of International Law and a member of the Board of Editors of the *American Journal of International Law*.

Adrian S. Fisher is Dean of the Georgetown Law Center. He was formerly Deputy Director of the U.S. Arms Control and Disarmament Agency, Vice-President and Counsel of the Washington *Post*, Legal Advisor of the Department of State, and General Counsel for the Atomic Energy Commission.

Victor Gilinsky, a member of the Physics Department Research Staff of the Rand Corporation, received his Ph.D. degree in Theoretical Physics from the California Institute of Technology in 1961. He is a past consultant to IDA International and Social Studies Division and is a member of the American Society for the International Law Panel on Nuclear Energy and World Order.

Henry R. Myers, President and principal consultant of Myers Associates, Inc., received the S.B. degree from the Massachusetts Institute of Technology in 1954 and the Ph.D. degree in Physics from the California Institute of Technology in 1960. Prior to establishing Myers Associates, he was experimental physicist at the Harvard-MIT Cambridge Electron Accelerator and Physical Science Officer at the U.S. Arms Control and Disarmament Agency.

John Gorham Palfrey is Professor of Law at Columbia University. He was formerly Commissioner of the U.S. Atomic Energy Commission and a Fellow of the Kennedy Institute of Politics, Harvard University.

George W. Rathjens, Jr., Professor of Political Science at the Massachusetts Institute of Technology, received his Ph.D. degree in Chemistry from the University of California. Mr. Rathjens has held the positions of Director of the Weapons Systems Evaluation Division and Director of the Systems Evaluation Division with the Institute of Defense Analyses. He is the author of *The Future of the Strategic Arms Race: Options for the 1970's* (1969).

Lawrence Scheinman is Associate Professor of Political Science at the University of Michigan. The present study was prepared during Mr. Scheinman's tenure as Visiting Research Scholar of the Carnegie Endowment for International Peace. Mr. Scheinman's previous publications in the field of nuclear policy include: *Atomic Energy Policy in France Under the Fourth Republic*, and the articles "EURATOM: Nuclear Integration in Europe," and "Nuclear Safeguards, the Peaceful Atom, and the IAEA."

Herbert Scoville, Jr., is Director, Arms Control Program, Carnegie Endowment for International Peace. Mr. Scoville served as Assistant Director for Scientific Intelligence and later as Deputy Director for Research with the CIA and as Assistant Director, Science and Technology, of the U.S. Arms Control and Disarmament Agency. He is the co-author of *Missile Madness* (1970).